全国高等教育商务英语规划系列教材

商务英语写作教程
A Coursebook for Business English Writing

主　编　李太志
副主编　董　坤

- 体验商贸交流过程
- 锤炼商贸交流技能
- 培养商务写作意识

以问题为导向的教学理念
对传统信函进行的升级改造

苏州大学出版社

图书在版编目(CIP)数据

商务英语写作教程 = A Coursebook for Business English Writing / 李太志主编. —苏州：苏州大学出版社，2022.1
全国高等教育商务英语规划系列教材
ISBN 978-7-5672-3861-9

Ⅰ.①商… Ⅱ.①李… Ⅲ.①商务-英语-写作-高等学校-教材 Ⅳ.①F7

中国版本图书馆 CIP 数据核字(2022)第 005107 号

书　　名：	商务英语写作教程
	A Coursebook for Business English Writing
主　　编：	李太志
策划编辑：	汤定军
责任编辑：	汤定军
装帧设计：	吴　钰
出版发行：	苏州大学出版社（Soochow University Press）
社　　址：	苏州市十梓街 1 号　邮编：215006
印　　刷：	常熟市华顺印刷有限公司
邮购热线：	0512-67480030
销售热线：	0512-67481020
开　　本：	787 mm×1 092 mm　1/16　印张：11.75　字数：279 千
版　　次：	2022 年 1 月第 1 版
印　　次：	2022 年 1 月第 1 次印刷
书　　号：	ISBN 978-7-5672-3861-9
定　　价：	42.00 元

凡购本社图书发现印装错误，请与本社联系调换。服务热线：0512-67481020
苏州大学出版社网址　http://www.sudapress.com
苏州大学出版社邮箱　sdcbs@suda.edu.cn

全国高等教育商务英语规划系列教材

顾　问　徐青根　鲁加升

编　委　（以姓氏笔画为序）

于延梅	王　娅	王　翔	王红华
王金华	王德丽	毛卫强	文　格
方小勇	朱冬梅	刘　萱	孙亚玲
孙志祥	李卫东	李太志	李甜甜
杨　晓	步阳辉	张　莹	张　涛
张夏菲	陈　羔	陈　培	陈东东
林又佳	季　宇	金焕荣	郑　骏
施　翔	姚春宁	姚菊霞	袁海燕
顾　红	顾　薇	顾秀梅	徐　健
徐　源	董　坤	程进军	曾　艳
潘　珺	穆连涛		

策　划　汤定军

前言

在经贸全球化（globalization）与一体化（integration）进程日益加快的今天，我国与世界各国之间的商贸活动日益频繁，对外商贸业务不断扩大，人们越来越多地使用英语这个最常用的国际商务工作语言，进行商贸交流与沟通。随着商贸交流与沟通的范围和方式的扩展，商务英语写作涉及的商贸业务知识和惯例、传递信息的手段和方式及使用语言的表达习惯都在发生变化。《商务英语写作教程》作为商务英语专业的教材，正是为满足广大商务英语学习者对培养和提高商务英语写作能力的需要而编写的。

商务英语学习者需要熟悉并掌握的专业技能之一就是有效而得体的商务英语书面沟通与交流技能。熟悉并掌握商务英语书面沟通与交流技能的重要途径就是对商贸书面交际过程的专业体验（Experience & Practice）、对商务写作技能的训练（Writing Skills）和对商务英语写作修辞意识的研讨（Comment & Improvement），由此而获得真实或近似真实的切身感受，并培养和提高有效商务英语写作修辞意识和能力。

众所周知，要写好商务英语应用文，首先要有一定的英语写作水平；其次，应熟悉和掌握各种商务英语应用文文体的写作修辞要求、写作修辞倾向、写作修辞方法等。此外，更要了解商务写作与一般性写作之间的区别；经过反复地学习、模仿和套用，才能逐步掌握商务英语应用文的写作修辞方法与技能，逐步学会撰写各类商务英语应用文，以此进行富有成效的商贸书面沟通与交流。

对于广大商务英语专业和国际贸易专业的学生而言，专业技能和实践经验是他们就业求职时企业十分看重的关键因素，然而这是他们有待加强的薄弱环节，也是提高高等教育质量的重要方面。

本书的第一大亮点是，对大量实例的体验、对案例的分析和对写作技能的训练，旨在为学习者提供可能面临的商贸情景的范例，帮助学习者对商贸情景中常用文体的格式有一个总的了解，从而能尽快掌握商贸书面沟通技巧及常用的商务写作方法，提高使用英语进行商贸书面交流与沟通的能力，使他们在商务英语写作中举一反三、得心应手，从事商贸活动更加顺利。

本书的第二大亮点是，紧跟当今教育教学思想与理念，以商务英语写作中出现的较为典型的问题为导向开展研讨并加以修改完善，以培养分析问题和解决问题的能力为目标，培养敏感的有效商务英语写作修辞意识与专业的书面沟通技能。

本书的第三大亮点是，运用现当代国际商务英语写作的原则和方法，对充斥大量陈词滥调与冗词赘句的传统信函进行现代化升级改造，去旧（删除那些老套迂腐的用语）换新，化繁（去掉那些冗词赘句和语义过虚的用词）为简，使其更加符合现当代商务英语写作标准与要求。

本书的特色就在于贯穿和统领全书全过程的体练精神。每单元先提供专业知识和商贸书面交流要点的介绍，后以写作实例的形式进行商贸交流与谈判的英语（对话和信函/备忘录/报告）奉献于学习者面前，使他们能够切身体验近似真实的商贸业务过程和地道规范的商贸交流方式；继而进行大量与商务英语交流与沟通技能相关的训练和商务英语写作修辞意识的研讨培养，以此达到熟悉商贸业务过程、掌握商贸交际技能和培养商务英语写作修辞意识之目的。

本书主要包括两大部分，共15单元。第一部分是对外交流及其商务英语信函写作，第二部分为企业内部交流及其商务英语写作。每个单元基本由以下三个板块组成：商贸业务书面交流的体验感受、商务英语交流技能的训练和商务英语写作修辞意识的研讨培养。由此可见，本书是集业务体验、技能训练与意识研讨为一体的实用而易于操作的商务英语写作教材。

本书适用于从事国际商贸活动的白领阶层、经常用英语进行书面沟通的其他人士及即将毕业并有志于从事国际商贸活动的大中专院校的学生，既可供高等院校英语专业、商务英语专业和国际经济与贸易专业学生作为教材使用，也可作为想了解商务英语写作的其他人士的参考资料。

最后，谨向本书参考研究成果的专家学者致以衷心的感谢！同时，恳请对本书存在的疏漏之处给予批评指正。

李太志

2021年11月

Contents

■ **Part One   External Communication & BE Writing**

Unit 1   Components & Layouts of BE Letters   3

1.1   Understanding the Essential & Optional Components
        of BE Letters   4
1.2   Laying Out Business English Letters   12
1.3   Writers' Workshop: Awareness for Effective BE
        Practical Writing   17

Unit 2   Asking to Establish Business Relations & Replies   20

2.1   Experience & Practice   20
2.2   Communicating & Writing Skills   24
2.3   Writers' Workshop: The Process of Writing   29

Unit 3   Credit Enquiries & Replies   32

3.1   Experience & Practice   32
3.2   Communicating & Writing Skills   36
3.3   Writers' Workshop: Businesslike Poise & Formal Style   39

Unit 4   Enquiries & Replies   42

4.1   Experience & Practice   42
4.2   Communicating & Writing Skills   46
4.3   Writers' Workshop: Opening & Closing a Letter   51

Unit 5 Quotations, Offers & Counter-offers — 54

5.1	Experience & Practice	54
5.2	Communicating & Writing Skills	59
5.3	Writers' Workshop: Proposition vs Counter-proposition	64

Unit 6 Orders & Replies — 66

6.1	Experience & Practice	66
6.2	Communicating & Writing Skills	72
6.3	Writers' Workshop: Textual Development of Letters (1)	75

Unit 7 Payment & Replies — 79

7.1	Experience & Practice	79
7.2	Communicating & Writing Skills	84
7.3	Writers' Workshop: Textual Development of Letters (2)	90

Unit 8 Shipment & Replies — 92

8.1	Experience & Practice	92
8.2	Communicating & Writing Skills	96
8.3	Writers' Workshop: Principles for BE Writing	99

Unit 9 Packing & Replies — 102

9.1	Experience & Practice	102
9.2	Communicating & Writing Skills	106
9.3	Writers' Workshop: Concreteness vs Abstractness	109

Unit 10 Insurance & Replies — 111

10.1	Experience & Practice	111
10.2	Communicating & Writing Skills	115
10.3	Writers' Workshop: Qualities of Effective Sentence Writing	117

Unit 11	Claims & Adjustments	119
11.1	Experience & Practice	119
11.2	Communicating & Writing Skills	122
11.3	Writers' Workshop: Create an Appropriate Tone	125

Unit 12	Agency	127
12.1	Experience & Practice	127
12.2	Communicating & Writing Skills	131
12.3	Writers' Workshop: Conciseness & Simplicity	134

Unit 13	Social Letters	136
13.1	Experience & Practice	136
13.2	Communicating & Writing Skills	141
13.3	Writers' Workshop: Completeness vs Incompleteness	145

■ Part Two   Internal Communication & BE Writing

Unit 14	Memorandums	149
14.1	Experience & Practice	149
14.2	Communicating & Writing Skills	153
14.3	Writers' Workshop: Trend for Contemporary BE Letter Writing	155

Unit 15	Business Reports	158
15.1	Experience & Practice	159
15.2	Communicating & Writing Skills	164
15.3	Writers' Workshop: Accuracy & Objectivity	167

Appendixes	170

References	175

Part One

External Communication & BE Writing

Learning Objectives

✓ understanding the essential and optional components of BE letters
✓ learning about the three most common layouts of BE letters
✓ laying a letter out in the right way
✓ learning about the writing process

Identify Problems in the Following Writing & Comment

The International Trading Corporation
Dalian 116025, Liaoning Province
93 Green Avenue, China
2021/5/15
Gold & Silver
372 West 7th Street
Paris 10094
Ref: Inquiry about Washing Machines
Dear Sirs,
Attention: Sales Department
Some years ago we bought from you a consignment of washing machines in 2 different qualities. Please let us know whether you are still manufacturing washing machines in these qualities and quote your lowest price C. I. F. Dalian.
We should require delivery within 4 weeks of placing the order.
Yours faithfully,
Michel Johnson
Sales manager
The International Trading Corporation

1.1 Understanding the Essential & Optional Components of BE Letters

1.1.1 Looking at the names of the different components of a business letter in the box and putting them under the appropriate headings: Essential Components or Optional Components

Essential Components	Optional Components

letter-head   reference numbers   inside name and address
attention line   salutation   subject line
body of the letter   complimentary close   signature
identification initials   enclosure notation   C. C. line
P. S. notations   date

1.1.2 Learning about the essential & optional components of BE letters

☞ **A. Read and complete the following descriptions of the essential components of BE letters.**

a. The letter-head is the name and address of the firm which writes the letter. It tells where the letter comes from and it is also called _____. It is the most obvious part of a business letter and usually put at the topmost position so as to give the addressee a very first impression. A letter-head may contain some or all of the following parts: the company name, _____, telephone numbers, fax numbers, e-mail address, and logo (the company symbol). For example,

Example 1:

> EASTERN TEXTILES IMP. & EXP. CO., LTD.
> 12389 Changchun Road, Dalian, China
> Tel: (0411) 8660#####   Fax: (0411) 8650####
> http://will.nease.net
> E-mail: bcxbcx@411cn.com

Unit 1 Components & Layouts of BE Letters

Example 2:

> **SINOCHEM GROUP**
> 11/F, Central Tower, Chemsunny World Trade Center, 28 Fuxingmennei Street, Beijing 100031
> The People's Republic of China
> Tel: 0086 - 10 - 59568888   Fax: 0086 - 10 - 59568890

b. The date tells when the writer writes the letter and it is a vital item in a business letter. Under the printed letterhead, you can type the _____ in full, in the logical order of day, month and year. That is the British English arrangement of the date, but in _____, the month comes first and the date follows. The position of the date depends on the style you adopt. When writing on blank paper, type the name of your firm, its address, and the date at the right or left margin, depending on the style you choose. In British correspondence, the date is on the right and could be after the inside address. And there is a growing tendency to omit the -th, -rd, -nd and -st that follow the day. For example,

15 October, 2021 (British English)
October 15, 2021 (American English)

c. The inside name and address contains the name and the address of the _____, the person or company you are writing to. It is on the _____, two spaces below the date line. If you know the name and title of the person, you should include them. In addressing an individual in a company, the inside address contains both the individual's name and that of the company. The address should be the same as the one on the _____.

Courtesy titles are used in business letters. "Mr", "Ms", "Mrs" or a substitute form should never be omitted from the inside address. When writing to a woman always address her as she signs herself. It is considered correct to address a woman "Ms" unless she has signed herself "Mrs".

"Esquire" or "Esq." may be used in addressing prominent attorneys or other high-ranking professional men who do not have other titles. "Esq." always follows the name, separated from it by a comma. "Mr" does not precede the name when "Esquire" or "Esq." is used. For example,

John, Esq.

Other common titles include "Prof." and "Dr." which are _____ titles, and "Rev." (reverend) and "Hon." (honorable) which are used for senators, congressmen, ambassadors, governors, judges, mayors, and heads of government departments, etc.

"Mr" or "Esq." is used in England for addressing a single man while "Messrs." (plural form of Mr) may be used in addressing a firm of men, or men and women, when the name includes a personal element. For example,

Messrs. Barringtan Bros. Ltd. (柏林坦兄弟公司)
Messrs. Waterman & Co. (华胜曼公司)
Messrs. Brown & Brown Pacific Insurance Services (布朗&布朗太平洋保险公司)

A Coursebook for Business English Writing

d. The salutation is the greeting to the reader. It should be typed flush with the _____ margin, two spaces below the last line of the inside address. The most common salutation consists of "Dear" plus the recipient's name.

As the use of the first name in salutation is an _____ practice, it is not recommended for formal commercial correspondence. We do not usually use both the first and the last name in the salutation. But it is acceptable to use the full name such as "Dear John Smith" in a salutation, especially when the writer cannot determine the gender of the recipient.

If the writer has no idea of the identification of the addressee(s), "To Whom It May Concern", "Dear Sir", "Dear Sir or Madam" or "Dear Sirs" (American English: Gentlemen) is often employed in a business letter. For example,

Dear Mr. Stevenson,
Dear Messrs. White & Son Co. Ltd.,
Dear Sirs,
Gentlemen,
To Whom It May Concern,

e. As the message that the writer has to convey to the addressee, the body of the letter is the most important part of a letter. It begins two spaces below the salutation. The body of the letter may consist of one paragraph only, or of as many paragraphs as needed. If the message is very short, it is advisable to arrange the message in at least 2 paragraphs. But when the message is too long to fit into one page, the _____ can be continued onto the second page, which should carry at least 2 lines. On each continuation page, the name of the addressee, the page number and the _____ should be typed in either of the following two ways.

Mrs Green   2   January 26, 2008
Or:
Mrs Green
Page 2
January 26, 2008

There should be margin at least one inch on both sides of the paper, at the top, and at the bottom. If your letter is very short, you should make your margins larger.

There is single space between lines unless the letter is very short. _____ spaces are between paragraphs.

When the indented style is used, the first line of each paragraph is usually indented 5–8 letter spaces.

f. The complimentary close or closing _____ the letter. It is two spaces below the last line of the body. Capitalize only the first letter of the first word. Begin it slightly to the right of the center of the page except in the block style.

There are many ways to write the complimentary close or closing. "Yours sincerely" is most commonly used. "Sincerely" is the most popular complimentary close in America. "Yours faithfully" is British usage in a letter with "Dear Sir" or "Dear Sirs" as salutation. Other formal salutations are "Yours truly" and "Yours respectfully". The complimentary close you write in a letter depends on the _____ you use at the beginning. But the trend today is to use the less _____ forms of complimentary closes in business letters, rather than the formal ones. The expression used must be suitable for the occasion and should reflect the writer's relationship with the addressee.

Examples of Different Styles:

Formal	Semi-formal	Informal	Personal
Yours faithfully,	Sincerely yours,	Best regards	Love
Yours truly,	Yours sincerely,	Kindest regards	With love
Faithfully yours,	Cordially yours,	Best wishes	Cheers
Respectfully yours	Sincerely,	Thanks	As always

g. As the absolutely necessary element of a BE letter, the signature is the signed name or mark of the person who writes the letter or the company which he or she represents. It is written in ink immediately below the _____. The name of company can be in typed form while the person who takes in charge of the business letter must sign his or her name legibly in ink. To sign with a rubber stamp is a form of _____.

Below is a sample letter to show the different components of a BE letter which are arranged in the block style:

Shanghai Chemicals Trading Co. Ltd.
8 Fuxing Road
Shanghai 200030, China
Tel: 021-61000000   Fax: 021-61000001

May 17, 2020

Mr. Ichiju Tanaka
Deputy General Manager
Fuji Trading Co. Ltd.
Yamashita-cho, Naka-ku
Yokohama
Japan

Dear Mr Tanaka,

Your consignment of chemicals is now ready for dispatch and we are arranging shipment by S. S. Yamagawa Maru, sailing from Shanghai on May 24.

A Coursebook for Business English Writing

> The sulfuric acid is supplied in thirty 4-gallon carboys and with a protective lid to avoid breakage of the mouth. The ammonia is in forty 5-cwt steel drums.
>
> Please confirm safe arrival of the consignment.
>
> Sincerely yours,
>
> *Zhang Hao*
>
> Zhang Hao

B. Read the description of the optional parts of BE letters and answer the questions below.

a) What is the function of the reference numbers, the attention line and the subject line?

b) What are the identification initials? And what are the CC line and the PS line?

The optional or additional parts may be included in commercial correspondence. They are special parts of a letter that supply data for the benefit of the writer or for the information of the addressee, or for the use of them both. Some optional parts are placed near the top of the letter and some near its bottom. The additional parts include the reference numbers, the attention line, the subject line, the identification initials, the enclosure notation, the C.C. line and the P.S. notation, etc.

a. Reference numbers enable replies to be linked with earlier correspondence and ensure that they reach the right person or department without delay. For example,

> **New Japan Chemical Co., Ltd.**
> 2-1-8, Bingo-machi, Chuo-ku, Osaka 541-0051
> Japan
> Tel: 81-06-62020624
>
> Our ref: PL/fh/246
> 12 January 1987
>
> Dear Mr Basuki,
>
> This is to introduce ourselves as a leading chemical company having developed advanced technologies for high-pressure reactions, organic synthesis and oxidation reactions. We are writing to you with a view to building business relationship with you.
>
> To give you a general idea of our products available now for export, we are enclosing a catalogue and a price list for your information.
>
> If you are interested in any of our products, please let us know. We shall be pleased to give you our lowest quotations upon receiving your detailed requirements.
>
> We look forward to receiving your favorable reply.
>
> Yours sincerely
> [Signature]

b. The attention line is used when the writer of the letter addressed to a company wishes to get it delivered or directed to a particular person or the proper department.

The attention line always follows the inside address and precedes the salutation. It may be typed flush with the left margin or centered on the page. It is written either in all capital letters or underlined. For example,

Attention: Marketing Department
Attention of Personnel Department
For the attention of Mr Wang Dawei

Sample Letter Showing Position of Attention Line:

Macdonald & Evans Co. Ltd.
58 Lawton Street, New York, U. S. A.

August 20, 2006

Fujian Shoes Import & Export Corporation
45 Baoding Street, Fuzhou
Fujian, China
Attention: Sales Department

Dear Sirs,

  We have obtained your name and address from Fort & Co. Ltd. and we are writing in the hope that you would be willing to establish business relations with us.

  We have been leading importers of casual shoes for many years. At present, we are interested in extending our range and appreciate your catalogs and quotations.

  If your prices are competitive, we would like to place a trial order with you.

  We look forward to your early reply.

Yours sincerely,
Macdonald & Evans Co. Ltd.
Michael Evans
Michael Evans
Manager

  c. The subject line of a letter is used when the writer wants to tell the reader the subject of the letter. The subject line always follows the salutation and precedes the body of a letter. It may be typed flush with the left margin or centered on the page. When both an attention line and a subject line are included in a letter, follow the same typing style for each. The introductory word or phrase is always followed by a colon. For example,

Subject: Delay of Payment
Re: Proposed delay of the shipment
SUBJECT: LETTER OF CREDIT NO. 2472

  The above-mentioned optional parts are just notations near the top of the letter while the following notations are near its bottom.

d. Identification initials identify the writer of the letter and the person who types it. They are mainly used for administrative purposes. The initials of the signer come first, in all capital letters, followed by the initials of the typist, separated either by a slash(/) or a colon. Identification initials are usually typed flush with the left margin two spaces below the signature. For example,

AS/hu

or:

AS:hu

e. A writer who is enclosing anything in the letter should indicate this in the letter body by saying:

We are enclosing ...
We enclose ...
Enclosed is ...
Please find enclosed ...
Enclosed please find ...

The word, "Enclosure", is self-descriptive. It means that the material other than the letter itself is enclosed. Below the signature, or below the identification initials if there should be, the writer who is enclosing anything in the letter should indicate this by using the word, "Enclosure" or its abbreviation "Enc", "Encl" or "encl". It is typed flush with the left margin.

f. Copies of the letter may be sent to various people, who need to know about the message even though it doesn't pertain to them directly. These may be carbon copies, but most probably they will be photocopied. The notations of "Copies to", "C" (copy), "CC" (carbon copy), "PC" (photocopy), or "XC" (Xerox copy) designate that others are receiving copies.

g. "Per Pro" or "PP" is the abbreviation of "per procurationem", which is a Latin phrase denoting agency. Strictly speaking, only the partner is entitled to sign the name of his firm, but for the sake of convenience, authority to sign is often given to a responsible employee by a document known as a power of attorney, though the authority to sign may also arise from custom.

h. P. S. line is an afterthought or an extra message added at the end of the letter. In formal letters, it is usually a sign of poor planning. But as a piece of special advice, it has two legitimate functions. To add a personal touch to their typewritten letter, some executives occasionally add a postscript in pen and ink. And writers of sales letters often withhold one last convincing argument for emphasis in a postscript. For example,

P. S. Wish to get your reply on March 8 latest.
P. S. ... to see you at the Annual Sales Meeting at the Hillside Plaza on January 10.
P. S. I understand that the special entertainment is great.

Unit 1 Components & Layouts of BE Letters

1.1.3 Practice

A. Here are some common ways to write the salutation. Now fill in the form below with the salutations given in the box.

Dear Madam	To Whom It May Concern	Dear Sir	Dear Sirs (*BrE*)
Gentlemen (*AmE*)	Dear John	Dear Mr Smith	Dear Miss Smith
Dear Mrs Smith	Dear Ms Smith		

To Whom	Salutation
to a company	
to a man if you do not know his name	
to a woman if you do not know her name	
to a man	
to a married woman	
to an unmarried woman	
to a married or unmarried woman	
to a friend or someone you know well	
to sb whose gender the writer doesn't konw	

B. Read the different components numbered ①–⑪ of the following letter and select one of the three layouts to put them in the right order.

① THE EASTERN SEABOARD CORP
350 Park Avenue
New York, New York 10017
Telephone: 225-2780; Fax: 225-2711

② Kanto Mercantile Corporation
2-1, Nihonbashi 3-chome, Chuo-ku
Tokyo 101
JAPAN

③ Your Ref.: 4379
Our Ref.: 3456

④ Attention: Mr Makio Abe, Export Manager

⑤ Subject: New Price List

⑥ Gentlemen,

⑦ Thank you for your friendly and interesting letter of February 25. Although the new pricelist arrived yesterday, we are glad to tell you that it came just in time for our needs.

⑧ Sincerely yours,

⑨ THE EASTERN SEABOARD CORP

⑩ *James Parrinton*
James Parrinton
Vice President

⑪ February 26, 1986

12　A Coursebook for Business English Writing

☞ **C. Read the following letter and point out the different parts that compose it in the order of arranging the components.**

May 22, 2001

Fred Flintstone
Sales Manager
Cheese Specialists Inc.
456 Rubble Rd.
Rockville, IL 89675

Dear Mr Flintstone,

Thank you for your phone call of 3rd January. I am pleased to hear that Model BHT43 has been selling well. I am attaching a leaflet listing our full range of lawnmowers, as requested.

I look forward to doing business further with you in the future.

Yours sincerely,
Fred Flintstone
Fred Flintstone

1.2　Laying Out Business English Letters

1.2.1　Learning about the layouts of BE letters

☞ **A. Brief introduction**

Questions *What is the most convenient and popular style? Why?*

　　There are three common layouts of business English letters. They are the full block style, the modified block style and the conventional indented style.

　• The full block and the modified block style

　　The full block style, an American style, has now come to be much more widely used than before. Now, it is used in more than 80% of all business English letters. Its striking feature is that all of the typing lines of a letter are flush with the left-hand margin. The open punctuation pattern used in the block style requires that the end of the date line, the inside address lines, the salutation, the complimentary close and the signature lines are unpunctuated.

　　The modified block style is a combination of the indented style and the block style. It is also called semi-block style or mixed-block style. As an eclectic style, it is most widely used in international business letter writing. And it is to cater for the older readers' taste for the composition of a business letter and as a result, more writers begin to use the modified block style.

In both the full block and the modified block style, the new paragraph needn't be indented as there are double spaces between paragraphs. Therefore, the full block and the modified block style are convenient to type.

- The conventional indented style

Of the three types, the indented style is the conventional and the most formal one. It is a traditional British practice with the heading usually centralized on the very top and the date line on the right-hand side. The complimentary closing may be in the center or start at the central point. The first line of each paragraph in the body of the business letter is indented 5 – 8 letter spaces. The indented style looks good but it is not convenient to type.

B. Read and answer the following questions.

a) Are all of the following letters laid out in the same way? What have you noticed about the layouts of the following letters?

b) Where's the date in the following letters? On the right or on the left?

c) Are the paragraphs of all the following letters aligned with the left margin?

d) Are there 2 spaces between paragraphs?

Letter 1

77 Eastern Road
Chiswick
London
UK
Telephone 45632
Fax 68539

November 26, 2002

Mr Pierre Dupont
Managing Director
Dupont Freres
4 Rue de la Paix
Paris 16
France

Dear Mr Dupont,

Subject: Offer of the Summer Discount of 20%

I enjoyed touring your company last week. Thank you so much for giving me the opportunity to demonstrate the new Handi-Jack tool belt.

I checked with the distribution center about your question on bulk orders. Yes, I can still offer you the summer discount of 20% off each large business shipment. (Offer expires December 31, 2002.)

A Coursebook for Business English Writing

I look forward to hearing from you.

Sincerely yours,
Sandra Jones
Sandra Jones
Sales Manager

Letter 2

BUSINESS CORRESPONDENCE INSTITUTE
Hui Zong An, Beijing, China
Tel: 010 –68234171 **Fax**: 010 –68234173

Our ref:
Your ref:

June 7, 1986

Mr K. Huang
65 Nathan Road
Kowlon
HONG KONG

Dear Mr Huang,

You asked me if there is any one letter-style that is used more than the others. Probably more business concerns use the modified block style, because it saves time for the typist. However, many companies are adopting the block style, as it saves even more time than the modified block style. This letter is an example of the modified block style. As you can see, the inside name and address are blocked and paragraphs' beginnings are aligned with the left margin, as they are in the block style. Open punctuation is used in the inside address.

The date and reference lines are flush with the right margin. The complimentary close begins slightly to the centre of the page. Both lines of signature are aligned with the complimentary close.

Yours sincerely,
T. V. Li
T. V. Li
President

Unit 1   Components & Layouts of BE Letters   15

Letter 3

EuroCom
European Communications Company
16 Bedford Road   London W4 1HV
Tel: 0180 783 9576   Fax: 0181 792 3434

March 3, 2021

Dear Sir or Madam,

<u>Different Ways of Communicating in Writing</u>

In a letter, the emphasis is on a high-quality appearance. Letters have to be typed or word-processed accurately on the company's headed paper with a smart, clear layout. International mail tends to be slow and in some countries the post is unreliable. Important documents and valuable items can be sent by registered mail or they can be sent by courier.

A fax is a facsimile copy of a document which is transmitted by normal telephone lines to another fax machine. Some faxes are exactly like letters, some are printed on special fax forms rather like memos, others are simply handwritten messages. The sender of a fax can't be certain if the message has been received perfectly—sometimes lines get missed or are illegible. A fax is not usually a legally binding document.

E-mail (electronic mail) is a way of sending messages between computers. The message appears on a screen and can be printed out if necessary. To make e-mail more personal, some people use punctuation to add happy (☺) or unhappy (☹) faces to their messages.

Internal mail within a company or between branches of the same firm is usually in the form of memos: these may be brief handwritten notes or longer, word-processed letters. Most firms use special memo pads for internal messages. A memo to a senior English-speaking member of staff may need as much care as a letter to a client. The style that is used depends on the practice within the company and on the relationship between the people involved.

Faithfully yours,
Edward Linch
Edward Linch

☞ **C. Read the following letter and complete it according to the Chinese given in the brackets.**

BUSINESS CORRESPONDENCE INSTITUTE
Hui Zong An, Beijing, China
Tel: 010 – 68234171   Fax: 010 – 68234173

June 7, 2021

Mr K. Huang
65 Nathan Road
Kowlon
HONG KONG

Dear Mr Huang,

I am very glad to tell you about the differences among _____a._____ (完全齐头式、改良式和缩行式).

> The full block and the modified block style are quite similar to one another. In the full block style, all parts of the letter are placed flush with the left margin and _____ b. _____ （段落不缩进）. In the modified block style, everything except the date, reference numbers, complimentary close and signature is placed flush with the left margin.
>
> The full block style might be the most fashionable, but it has long been customary to _____ c. _____ （将信按照缩行式进行排列）. Many people regard it as the most attractive of all letter styles. _____ d. _____ （齐头式的封内地址）is liked because it is compact and tidy. This style appeals to most readers. They like the indented paragraphing and claim that it makes for easy reading.
>
> Yours sincerely,
T. V. Li
T. V. Li
President

1.2.2 Practice

☞ **A. Rewrite the following extracts from letters, trying to lay them out more attractively and appropriately. Make your comments before you make any improvement upon them.**

①

I noticed your advertisement in the *Daily Planet* amd I would be grateful if you could send me further information about your products. My company is considering subcontracting some of its office services and I believe that you may be able to supply us with a suitable service. Looking forward to hearing from you. Yours faithfuly.

②

There are a number of queries that I would like to raise about your products and I would be grateful if you could ask a representative to get in touch with me with a view to discussing these queries and hopefully placing an order if the queries are satisfactorily answered. Yours faithfully.

☞ **B. There are some mistakes concerning paragraphing, layout, wording and grammar in the following letter. Please improve them.**

> GLOBAL LUBRICANTS CO. LTD.
P. O. Box 3259
XXXX, XXX
>
> The Manager
> Messrs. Clarke & Smith Co. Ltd.
> 68 High Street
> London EC 4
> England

Dear Sir,

    Just send us details of your lubricants which you advertised in *Business Week* November 10.

    We ask you to quote us all the items listed on the enclosed inquiry form and give your prices C. I. F. Shanghai. Please indicate delivery time, your terms of payment, packing methods, and discount details for regular purchases and large orders.

    Our annual requirements for lubricants are considerable, and we may be able to place substantial orders to you if your prices are competitive and your delivery is prompt.

    We are expecting your quotation.

                                    Yours faithfully,
                                    Ross Camery
                                    Manager
                                    Your ref: TD/4812
                                    Our ref: EA/2719
                                    Encl: 2 catalogue
                                    3 price-lists
                                    January 22, 2021

1.3 Writers' Workshop: Awareness for Effective BE Practical Writing

Awareness for Effective BE Practical Writing

    One of the surprisingly sad facts is that many textbooks for BE practical writing in China are full of sample letters which are composed of long and complicated sentences made up of long and learned words. And some of the popular theories for BE letter writing still advocate the use of the formal style in writing long sentences and using hackneyed and stereotyped words and expressions of greater length than is required. As the BE learners are greatly impressed and affected by the above BE letter writing style, the natural effect is that they tend to write very long sentences by using very formal words without knowing that they belong to the traditional BE writing style and that they should have been thrown away into waste-paper baskets. In order that they can be exposed to the appropriate and effective BE practical writing style characterized by plentiful use of short sentences and short words which naturally lead to building a sweet tone in communication, the BE learners should be told about the necessity and importance for developing the awareness for effective and efficient BE practical writing.

    Awareness for effective BE practical writing is just the consciousness made up of the ideas about what are the appropriate principles and rules for effective and efficient BE practical writing and the abilities of knowing how to apply the right approaches and tones in BE practical writing. In detail, the awareness for effective BE practical writing is gradually acquired by learning how to distinguish and select the right sound, spelling, word, phrase, sentence, voice, tone, approach, organization of text, principle, etc. from more than forty opposite pairs. Awareness for effective BE practical writing seems to be abstract, but it is a concrete consciousness as is shown in the above. Below are some of the opposite pairs on lexical and syntactic dimension for the writers to make rhetorical optimization in BE practical writing.

Pairs of Opposite Rhetorical Phenomena & Language Forms on Lexical and Syntactic Dimension		
long words	vs	short words
learned words	vs	popular words
static words	vs	dynamic words
single verbs	vs	phrasal verbs
fml words	vs	infml words
abstract	vs	concrete
redundant	vs	concise
archaisms	vs	words in contemporary use
long sentences	vs	short sentences
compound/complex sentences	vs	simple sentences

1.3.1 Group work

Work in groups of three or four to select the appropriate words or expressions and discuss the different effects for the use of learned and popular words or expressions in the following letter.

Dear Sirs,
　　Your name has been given to us as reference by Willing & Co. who wants to open an account with us.
　　We _____ (shall/should) be much obliged if you _____ (can/could) give us some information on their financial status and business activities. We are especially interested to know whether you think that a credit of US $100,000 can be _____ (given/granted) safely.
　　Any information _____ (you give us / given to us) will certainly be treated in strict confidence. _____ (We enclose / Enclosed is) an address and a stamped envelope for your reply.
　　_____ (Thank you in advance for your help. / We shall appreciate your help very much.)
　　　　　　　　　　　　　　　　　　　　　Yours sincerely,
　　　　　　　　　　　　　　　　　　　　　[Signature]
　　Encl: 1 stamped envelope

1.3.2 Comparing the following pairs of sentences and making your comment.

　　① a. Thank you for talking with me on the phone last week regarding job opportunities.
　　① b. I wish to take this opportunity to thank you for talking to me on the phone last week about job opportunities with your firm.
　　② a. We are sorry to tell you that we do not have in stock any of the articles you said in your order of November 15.
　　② b. In reply to your order of November 15, we regret to advise you that we do not have in stock any such articles as you described.
　　③ a. We are pleased to place an order for the products specified below: ...

Unit 1 Components & Layouts of BE Letters   19

③ b. We would like to place an order for the following products: ...

1.3.3 Comment and improvement

Read the following letter and make your comment before you make any improvement to make it more effective and appropriate.

Dear Mr Brown,

What an unexpected pleasure to hear from you after all this time! We thought you must have forgotten us since you placed your previous order with us three years ago.

May I take this opportunity of enclosing for your attention our new catalogue and price lists. One of the things you'll probably notice is that all the prices have gone up by 15% since your last order but still, never mind, everyone else's have gone up too—even yours I expect! Nevertheless, for your current order, we shall be delighted to supply you at the old price, so you're quite lucky.

Oh, another thing, I nearly forgot: you can contact us if you feel like it. The number is 998321, all right?

So, there we are, nice to be writing to you again.

Yours faithfully,
John Burke
Sales Director

Unit 2 Asking to Establish Business Relations & Replies

Learning Objectives

- ✓ learning about the ways to find new customers and enter into business relations
- ✓ learning how to ask to enter into business relations and make replies
- ✓ learning how to perform relative functions of language and communication
- ✓ learning about the writing process

Identify Problems in the Following Writing & Comment

Dear Sirs,

　　Thanks for your Letter of Credit No. E-102 amounting to US $1,050,000.00 issued in our favor through the Hong Kong & Shanghai Banking Corporation.

　　With regard to shipment, we are sorry to tell you that, in spite of strenuous efforts having been made by us, we are still unable to book space on a vessel sailing to Jakarta direct. The shipping companies here told us that, for the time being, there is no regular boat sailing between ports in China and Jakarta. Therefore, we find it very difficult, if it is not impossible, to ship these 10,000 metric tons of sugar to Jakarta direct.

　　In view of the difficult situation faced by us, we request you to amend the L/C to allow transshipment of the goods in Hong Kong where arrangements can easily be made for transshipment. Please trust that we will ship the goods to Hong Kong right upon receipt of the L/C amendment. Since this is something beyond our control, we shall thank you for your agreement to our request and your understanding of our position.

　　We are anxiously waiting for the amendment to the L/C.

Yours sincerely,
[Signature]

2.1 Experience & Practice

2.1.1 Learning about the ways to find new customers and enter into business relations

☞ **A. Brief introduction**

Questions: What are the channels through which a company can find a business partner? Can you suggest any other channels?

① Channels through Which to Find a Business Partner

The development and expansion of a business (a company or a factory or an enterprise) depends upon customers. "No customer, no business" is a saying well-known in the business circles, so the establishment of business relations is the fundamental step in starting and developing business.

To seek prospective or potential clients/customers and establish business relations is one of the most important measures for a newly established firm or an old one that wishes to expand its market and enlarge its business scope and trade volume. Usually a firm may approach its new business counterparts in a foreign country or obtain necessary information through the following channels:

- Surfing on the Internet and writing to potential clients directly;
- Attending all kinds of commodity fairs or exhibitions;
- Asking old clients or friends in the commercial circles to make introductions or recommendations;
- Sending trade groups or delegations abroad for business talks;
- Asking local Chambers of Commerce in foreign countries for help;
- Using trade directories of various countries & regions and writing directly;
- Asking embassies or consulates or banks to make introduction or recommendation;
- Opening branches or sales agencies abroad;
- Placing advertisements in newspapers or magazines or on TV, etc.

Of all these channels, communication in writing is the means most commonly used for setting up business relations. But how can you obtain all the necessary information about a new client when you are going to write a letter to establish business relations? Maybe you can seek the help of many sources such as periodicals, advertisements in newspapers, market investigations, self-introduction by merchants themselves, etc.

② Points to Remember

After obtaining the desired names and addresses of the firms from any of the above channels or sources, you may start sending letters to the parties concerned. Generally speaking, this type of letter should start by telling the addressee the following:

◇ How and where you get the name and address of the addressee's company;
◇ Your intention or desire of writing the letter;
◇ The lines of business handled in your company;
◇ The reference as to your company's financial status and integrity.

If you are the recipient of such a letter, you ought to answer it in full without the least delay and with courtesy so as to create goodwill and leave a good impression upon the reader.

B. Experience by Reading and Answering Questions.

a. Read the following letter and answer the questions given below.

- How does the writer get to know the addressee as a prospective purchaser?
- What does the writer say to make his request for establishing business relations? Can you think of any other possible sentences to make the request?

Dear Sir or Madam,

　　Your company has been introduced to us by one of our business partners as a prospective purchaser of china. As this item comes within our range of operations, we shall be pleased to enter into business relations with you at an early date.

　　To give you a general idea of the various kinds of china now available for export, we are enclosing a brochure and a price list. Quotations and samples will be airmailed to you after receiving your specific enquiry.

　　We are looking forward to your early reply.

Yours sincerely,
Hans Seitz
Hans Seitz

Encl: 1 brochure
　　　1 price list

---

b. Read the following reply and answer the following questions.
- Is the writer willing to enter into business relations with the addressee? Does the customer take specific interest in any of the addressee's products?
- What request does the writer make in the letter?

Dear Sir or Madam,

Re: Establishing Business Relations

　　We acknowledge with thanks the receipt of your letter of May 6, 2006 and take the pleasure of establishing business relations with your corporation.

　　Your textile products are so attractive that we are confident of securing large orders for you. We shall be obliged if you could send us quotations and sample books.

　　We look forward to your favorable reply.

Yours sincerely,
Hilton S. Jefferson
Hilton S. Jefferson

2.1.2 Practice

A. Read the following telephone conversation and on Mr Hanson's behalf, write a letter asking to enter into business relations. Mr Hanson asks the exporter to refer to the writer's Enquiry Note 6315 attached for details and says that they are expecting to receive the addressee's lowest quotation as soon as possible.

Mr Hanson:　Hello. This is Benjamin Hanson from a Pakistani company in Islamabad. Our company is one of the leading importers of electric goods in this

Wang Ming:	city. And we'd like to build up business relations with you. Hello. This is Wang Ming, sales manager from Shanghai Branch of China National Light Industrial Products Import & Export Corporation. We're very glad to learn that you want to set up business relations with us.
Mr Hanson:	I know that you specialize in light industrial goods. At present, we're interested in vacuum cleaners, which sell very well here in our city. And we'll write to you telling about the details when we have an idea of what we want.
Wang Ming:	You're welcome to ask about anything about our goods and place your first order with us.
Mr Hanson:	Thank you. If you quote us the best price, we shall be able to promote the sale of your goods.
Wang Ming:	Just take my word. The price we'll give you will be the lowest and you can sell at a big profit.
Mr Hanson:	That'll be fine. We'll write to you very soon.

☞ **B. Now read the following letter and write a reply by using the particulars given below.**

* *You are an international trading company and have operations in all main trading countries of Europe.*
* *You are distributing products successfully for several other large companies.*
* *You have offices in London, Paris and Madrid.*
* *Say that you are willing to be their distributor.*

Incoming Letter

February 16, 2008

Dear Sir or Madam,

We are looking for a company which can help us distribute our products in new markets.

We manufacture a wide range of chemical products. At present we export to Canada, but we would like to export to Europe.

Enclosed is our brochure which gives details of our company.

We look forward to hearing from you.

Sincerely yours,

John Smith

2.1.3 Case study & practice

You have been manager of a Chinese company dealing in fine teacups and saucers, coffee cups and saucers for many years. You have been exporting them to Europe, but you intend to extend your business to the USA. Write a letter to an American company and say:

- ◇ You obtain the American company's name from an advertisement in an American newspaper.
- ◇ You express your hope of establishing business relations with the American company.
- ◇ You make a brief self-introduction to your own company and offer to supply the necessary catalogue and price list.
- ◇ You express your expectation to receive a reply.

2.2 Communicating & Writing Skills

☞ **A. Read the following letter and learn to tell how and where to have obtained the name and address of the recipient's company.**

Dear Sirs,

    Through the courtesy of our Commercial Counselor's Office in Tokyo, we come to know the name and address of your firm, and we have learned that you are one of the largest food trading companies in Japan with offices or representatives in all major cities and towns in the country. We are also told that you are interested in doing business with China.

    Our company specializes in exporting various foods to Europe and the USA. Now we are considering to export our foods to Japan. So we are writing in the hope of establishing business relations with you.

    To give you a general idea of our various foods available now for export, we are enclosing a catalogue and a price list for your reference.

    If you are interested in any of our items, please let us know. We shall be pleased to give you our lowest quotations upon receiving your detailed requirements.

    We look forward to receiving your favourable reply.

                                                                          Yours sincerely,
                                                                        [Signature]

Encl: 1 catalogue
       1 price list

    Substitute the underlined parts in the following sentences with those given below in the box.

have learned by courtesy of	understood
have obtained your name and address from	recommended

Unit 2 Asking to Establish Business Relations & Replies

1) We <u>owe your name and address to</u> the Commercial Counselor's Office of your embassy in Beijing and are now writing to you for the establishment of business relations.
2) We <u>have been told by</u> Mr Edison that you are one of the leading importers of Chinese chemicals and pharmaceutics in your country. And we would like to establish trade relations with you.
3) Your firm has been <u>told</u> to us by Bank of China in Beijing. We would like to build up direct business relations with you.
4) We <u>noticed</u> from Zhejiang's Trade Directory that you are a large importer of home electrical appliances. We wish to enter into business relations with your company on the basis of equality and mutual benefit.

B. Read the following letter and learn how to make a brief self-introduction.

Dear Sirs,

We are indebted for your address to the Commercial Counselor's Office of the Algerian Embassy in Beijing. They informed us that you are in the market for various chemicals used in petrochemicals.

It's on this subject that we approach you today in the hope of establishing mutually beneficial trading relations.

We are a state-operated corporation handling exclusively the export and import of chemicals. In order to acquaint you with our line, we enclose here with a copy of our export list showing the main items that are now available. Should you need anything not mentioned on the list, we shall do everything necessary upon receipt of your detailed requirements to secure the said items for you.

In our trade with customers in the Asian-African countries, we always adhere to the principle of equality, mutual benefit and the exchange of needed goods. It is our hope, by joint efforts, to promote both business and friendship to our mutual advantage.

We look forward to receiving your inquiries soon.

                   Yours faithfully,
                   [Signature]

Encl: 1 copy of export list

Complete the following useful sentences by using the verbs in the box.

| enjoying | dealing | cover | connected | introducing |

1) We have the pleasure of _____ ourselves to you as a big state-operated corporation.
2) Being closely _____ with reliable suppliers here, we can do substantial export business with you.
3) Our activities _____ a wide range of commodities including electric and electronic appliances.

4) We are an experienced exporting company _____ primarily in computers and have good connections with local manufacturers here.

5) We are well established as a manufacturer of cameras and our products are _____ high reputation for their excellent quality.

☞ **C. Read the following letter and learn how to offer helpful information and make promises of favorable prices.**

Dear Sirs,

    We learnt your name and address from the Chamber of Commerce, Tokyo, who informed us that you are in the market for Personal Computers.

    We are one of the largest computer manufacturers in our country and have handled the products for nearly 10 years. We approach you today in the hope of establishing business relations with you and expect, by our joint efforts, to enlarge the range of our business.

    In order to give you some idea about our business lines, we enclose a copy of our illustrated catalogue covering the main items available at present. If you are interested in any of the items, please tell us by fax or e-mail. We'll give you our lowest quotations and try our best to comply with your requirements.

    Our customers are always satisfied with our products and the after-sale service. And we are confident that you will be satisfied too, after we do business together.

    Our bankers are the Bank of Tokyo, Japan. They can give you information about our credit standing.

    We are looking forward to your early reply.

                          Yours sincerely,

                           [Signature]

Complete the following sentences by using the verbs in the box.

| give | sending | sent | enclosing | enclosed |

1) For your reference we are _____ our latest illustrated catalogue together with the price list on selected goods which we believe would be of interest to you.

2) To acquaint you with the light industrial goods we handle, we are _____ you, by separate airmail, several pamphlets for your reference.

3) The enclosed catalogue will _____ you a good knowledge of the articles we are handling.

4) _____ are our catalogue and price list covering the complete line of goods.

5) Our latest price list will be _____ to you upon request.

D. Read the following reply and see how to express thanks and make expectations.

Letter 1

Dear Sirs,

Thank you for your letter of September 16 and we shall be pleased to enter into trading relations with you.

At your request, we are sending you, under separate cover, our latest catalogue and price list covering our exports.

Payment should be made by an irrevocable and confirmed letter of credit.

If you feel that business is possible, please contact us for specific offers.

Yours sincerely,
[Signature]

Letter 2

Dear Sirs,

Thank you for your letter of the 20th August. We are desirous to enter into business relations with your company.

Our shoe industry concentrates on designing and producing various traditional and vogue men's and women's shoes. We have developed and marketed a series of products such as slippers of EVA, indoor slippers, cotton slippers, embroidered slippers of new style, children's shoes and cotton shoes. We can satisfy different market needs both at home and abroad.

In compliance with your request, we are sending you, under separate cover, our latest catalogue and price list covering our export range available at present.

Should you be interested in any items, please let us know. We are looking forward to your specific inquiries.

Yours sincerely,
Wugang
Manager

Study the following expressions.

- Expressions used to express thanks:
  * Thank you for your letter of August 15.
  * Thanks for your letter expressing the hope of entering into business connections with us.
  * Thank you for your letter offering your services and we would like to discuss the possibility of expanding trade with you.
  * We thank you for your letter of September 16, and shall be pleased to enter into trading relations with you.

A Coursebook for Business English Writing

- Expressions used to make expectations:
  * We look forward to hearing from you.
  * If you feel that business is possible, please contact us for specific offers.
  * We shall always be very happy to hear from you and will carefully consider any proposal likely to lead to business between us.
  * If any of the items listed in the catalogue meets your interest, please let us have your specific enquiry, and our quotation will be sent to you without delay.

☞ **E. Read and observe the expression used to accept the request for establishing business relations.**

> Dear Mr Wright,
>
> Thank you for your letter of November 28 and we are willing to enter into business relations with you. We have been exporting all kinds of art and craft goods for more than 25 years and have many customers and friends throughout Europe and America.
>
> At your request, we are sending you by air the latest catalogue and price list of our products for your reference. If any of the items listed in the catalogue meets your interest, please let us have your specific enquiry, and our quotation will be sent to you without delay.
>
> Sincerely yours,
> K. M. Abduah

Complete the following sentences by using the verbs in the box. Pay attention to the verb form.

coincide with ours	be willing to enter into business relations
we would like to discuss	meet our interest
fall within our business activities	

1) Thank you for your letter of June 27 expressing your wish to enter into trade relations with us, which also _____.
2) Thank you for your letter offering your services and _____ the possibility of expanding trade with you.
3) We _____ with your firm on the basis of equality, mutual benefit and exchanging what one has for what one needs.
4) Your desire to establish direct business relations with us _____.
5) This article _____.

Unit 2 Asking to Establish Business Relations & Replies

☞ **F. Read and observe the expression used to decline the request for establishing business relations.**

Dear Mr Obama,
　　We have received your letter of July 3, 2006 and thank you for your interest in cooperating with us.
　　We regret to say that we have to decline your suggestions since we are no longer in the market for pharmaceutical chemicals and we have recently made the decision to import nutritious food.
　　If you have any newly developed nutritious foods, however, please let us know as we are always open to new opportunities.

　　　　　　　　　　　　　　　　　　　　Sincerely yours,
　　　　　　　　　　　　　　　　　　　　Mr Taylor

Translate the following sentences by using the words in the box.

| not in our line | used to import | unable to co-operate |

1) 现回复你们建立义务关系的来函,我们十分遗憾,不能与你们合作,因为……
2) 由于这种货不在我们经营范围之内,所以我们已经把你们的询价函转交给适当的公司。
3) 很遗憾,我们不能接受你方提议,因为我们以前进口硅片,但是我们现在出口硅片了。

2.3　Writers' Workshop: The Process of Writing

7 Steps for Planning a Letter
　　Before you write your letters, it is advisable for you to follow the 7 steps mentioned below:
1. Clarifying your aims: What is the purpose of this letter?
2. Collecting all the relevant information and documents: copies of previous correspondence, reports, figures, etc.
3. Arranging the points in order of importance. Decide which points are irrelevant and can be left out. Make rough notes.
4. Writing an outline in note form. Check it through considering these questions:
   - Have you left out any important points?
   - Can the order of presentation be made clearer?
   - Have you included anything that is irrelevant?
5. Writing a first draft.
6. Revising your first draft by considering these questions:
   - Information: Does it cover all the essential points? Is the information relevant, correct and complete?

- English: Are the grammar, spelling and punctuation correct?
- Style: Does it sound natural and sincere? Is it clear, concise and courteous? Will it give the reader the right impression? Is it the kind of letter you would like to receive yourself?
7. Writing, typing and dictating your final version.

2.3.1 Group work

Imagine that you have received the following letter. What would you do in writing a reply?

Dear Sir or Madam,

　　We are wholesale distributors of plumbing and heating supplies and are interested in your products shown in *China Foreign Trade*.

　　We would like to hear from you about the possibility of importing the merchandise from China. If we can work together in this line to our mutual benefit, we can arrange for one of our representatives to make a trip to China and visit your office in person.

　　Enclosed is our latest catalogue showing the items we carry at present. And we wish you would send us your complete catalogue and a price list quoting the best discount for quantity buying.

　　Thank you for your early reply.

Sincerely yours,
[Signature]

Work in groups of 3 or 4 and try to decide what to do first, second and so on.

a) Make a plan for the letter to be written.

b) Note down important/useful phrases.

c) Write a draft.

d) Make changes and corrections.

e) Check spelling, grammar, style and layout.

f) Read carefully the letter you have received.

g) Read the letter again.

h) Send the letter.

i) Produce a final version.

2.3.2 Writing a letter plan for the following business situation

　　You work for a manufacturer of lawnmowers. You have been told by Ms. Jason in a telephone call that your product, Model BHT43, has been selling well. You just offer to attach to your e-mail letter a leaflet listing your full range of lawnmowers, as requested. In the closing of the letter, you just express your goodwill of doing business further with her in the future.

Unit 2 Asking to Establish Business Relations & Replies

2.3.3 Comment and improvement

Read the following letter in the form of memo and make your comment and improvement.

Memorandum   File No. 2010 −19

Date: Tuesday
To: Everybody
From: Sally
Subject: Professional development training next week!

Dear Everybody:

Sry about the late notice, but there are two professional development training sessions next week and boss wants us to fill them up. On Mon. is "Designing Usable Forms", open to Analysts. Tues is "Writing for the Reader", open to all. Please register this week with me or Julia. Give us your info and we'll send the times and schedules to upper management so they'll be informed.

Thnks, all!

Sal

Unit 3 Credit Enquiries & Replies

Learning Objectives

- ✓ learning about why and how to make credit enquiries
- ✓ learning to make credit enquiries in writing
- ✓ learning how to make positive and negative comments on credit status
- ✓ learning how to reply to credit enquiries
- ✓ learning about businesslike poise and formal style

Identify Problems in the Following Writing & Comment

Thank you for your letter of 31 September. Very surprised and disappointed to hear that you had been experiencing problems with "Sunrise" microwave oven that you bought from our branch in Kowloon. We shall of course be pleased to give you a full refund of HK $2,195 if you could bring the machine into our Customer Service Section (address down below). We assure you that your experience is not common, and hope that we shall be able to serve you again in the near future.

3.1 Experience & Practice

3.1.1 Learning about the ways to make credit enquiries and reply to them

☞ **A. Brief introduction**

Questions: *What do you make status enquiries about? And why and how do you make status enquiries?*

① Six C's & Channels of Credit Inquiry

The credit inquiry is mainly concerned with the financial position/standing/status, commercial integrity/goodwill of a potential partner and its relationship with the bank and other companies. Technically speaking, what to be inquired about can be concluded as "Six C's" — character (honesty, integrity and business ethics), capacity (profitability), condition (market demand and supply condition), capital, country (political stability of the country) and currency (strictness of the currency control of the country).

Before or at the beginning of establishing business relationship and involvement in international business, the exporters and the importers need to go through credit enquiry. The credit enquiry is made mainly to avoid being cheated and protect traders' interest.

There are various ways of getting information on the financial position, credit status, reputation and business methods of the other firms with which the enquirer plans to enter into business relations. Traders may turn to business friends, old clients, banks, chambers of commerce, or enquiry agencies for help. The information obtained from a bank or from a chamber of commerce is generally most reliable. It's often best for traders to get the necessary information through your own bank.

② Points to Remember

When you write a credit inquiry, you ought to follow the following steps:

- Begin directly with the objective, indicating an inquiry about a certain company's credit.
- Include specific requests or questions about a certain company's credit.
- If a number of questions or requests are involved, list them by numbers, or leave a space between them.
- End with a promise that the writer will keep the credit information in confidence.

When you write a reply to a credit inquiry, you ought to follow the following plan:

- Begin by indicating that you are answering his/her inquiries about a certain company's credit.
- Express interest in the inquiry.
- If possible, preferably offer a suggestion about whether to offer credit or how much credit.
- End with a request that the addressee should keep the credit information in confidence.

B. Experience by Reading and Answering Questions.

a. Read the letter asking for credit information and answer the following questions.

- *Who does the writer ask for credit information? A bank or an agency? Whose credit information supplied is more reliable?*
- *What promise does the writer make to the bank?*

Dear Sir,

The Maryland Inc.

The subject company is now offering to represent us in the sale of our Sewing Machines, and has referred us to your bank for detailed information about its credit standing, business capacity and character. Would you please give us your frank opinion on these points regarding the company?

Any information you may give us will be treated strictly in confidence.

Yours respectfully,
[Signature]

b. Read the reply to credit enquiry and answer the following questions.
- *How is the information provided by the bank? Is it positive or negative?*
- *What does the writer stress in the end of the letter?*

Gentlemen,

<u>Re: The Maryland Inc.</u>

The subject company you enquired about by your letter of October 12, 2008 has been maintaining an account with us for the past twenty years, during which they have never failed to meet their obligation. Their balance sheets of recent years enclosed will show you that their import business in Sewing Machines has been managed and operated under a satisfactory condition.

We believe that they owe their reputable position among the wholesalers in our district to their steady and sincere way of conducting business.

Please note that this information is furnished without any responsibility on our part and should be held strictly confidential.

Yours sincerely,

[Signature]

3.1.2 Practice

A. Read the following telephone conversation and then on Mr Black's behalf, write a letter to the Bank of China, Shanghai Branch, making credit enquiry.

Mr Black: Well, the Singapore Chamber of Commerce tells us that you wish to import electric goods manufactured in Singapore. I think our products will sell well in your country. But could you please tell me your credit standing?

Mr Zhou: No problem. For our credit standing, please refer to the Bank of China, Shanghai Branch. It can provide you with the information about our business and finances.

Mr Black: Thank you for referring me to your bank. I think honesty is the key to a long and profitable business relation.

Mr Zhou: Well, when can I get your final decision?

Mr Black: Next Wednesday at the latest.

Mr Zhou: Okay, I hope I'll get good news from you. In any case, thank you for your consideration. Bye.

Mr Black: So long.

☞ **B. Complete the following letter according to the Chinese given in the brackets.**

Dear Sirs,

In reply to your letter of June 15, we wish to inform you that we have now received from Barclay Bank of London the information you request. The London Trading Co., Ltd. was founded in 1940 with a capital of £ 2,000,000. They specialise in the import and export of textiles. Their suppliers' business with them is found to have been satisfactory. We _____ ① _____ (认为与他们做生意的最高赊欠额为 50 万英镑). For larger transactions we suggest payment by sight L/C.

The above information is _____ ② _____ (严格保密) and is given _____ ③ _____ (我方不承担任何责任).

                 Yours sincerely,
                 [Signature]

3.1.3 Case study & practice

On behalf of Pelican Paper Ltd., you are now to write a reply to the following credit enquiry.

Incoming Letter

Pelican Paper Ltd.
College Court
College Road
London N21 3LL

                 15 November 2020

Dear Sir or Madam,

         Re: Wainman Ltd.

The above company has asked us to supply them on credit.

We would be grateful for any comment that you may have from your experience with this company. Any information that you supply will be kept strictly confidential.

We thank you for your cooperation and look forward to hearing from you.

                 Yours sincerely,
                 [Signature]

And you can refer to the following facts when you write a reply to the above credit enquiry:

- ◆ About a year ago an action was brought against Wainman by one of its suppliers for recovery of the sums due, though payment was recovered in full.
- ◆ Wainman's difficulties were due to bad management and in particular to overtrading.
- ◆ Most of Wainman's suppliers either give only very short credit for limited sums, or make deliveries on a cash basis.

3.2 Communicating & Writing Skills

☞ **A. Read and learn how to make requests about credit enquiries.**

> Dear Sirs,
>
>   We'd like to enquire into the financial and credit status of the Auto Engineering Co., Ltd. Their reference is the National Bank of Nigeria, Ibadan.
>
>   Would you please help us in this respect? And we can assure you that any information you may give us will be kept strictly in confidence.
>
>   Sincerely yours,
[Signature]

Fill in the blanks of the following sentences with the words or expressions given below in the box.

> We shall appreciate it if
> Would you please give us your frank opinion
> Would you consider
> We shall be most grateful for
> We would therefore appreciate it if you could let us have

1) _____ any information you can obtain for us.
2) _____ on these points regarding the company?
3) _____ you will let us have the information on its credit standing, business capacity and character.
4) _____ a credit of US $1,500.00 a reasonable risk?
5) _____ information about the financial and business standing of the above firm.

☞ **B. Read and learn to state why to make credit enquiries.**

> Dear Sirs,
>
>   Recently we have received an order for our goods to the value of £1,600.00 from a new customer William Baker & Sons. As we have not done any business with them in the past, we would like to know if you could provide us with any information concerning their financial and credit status.
>
>   Enclosed please find the address of the above firm. Any information you may provide will be treated as strictly confidential.
>
>   Your early reply is appreciated.
>
>   Yours sincerely,
[Signature]

Unit 3 Credit Enquiries & Replies

Translate the following sentences into English.

1）我们收到了伦敦 Freemen Brothers Company 突然发来的出价。你们现正与该公司做生意，该公司把你们的名称提供给了我方做证明人。

2）该主题公司现主动提出做我们缝纫机的销售代理，并要我们向你们银行了解有关他们资信状况、业务范围和性质的详细情况。

3）我们打算与之进行交易的公司要我们向你们了解他们的业务状况和信誉的具体情况。

☞ **C. Read and learn how to promise to keep the information in strict confidence.**

Dear Sirs,

Re: The London Trading Co., Ltd.

Since we are on the point of concluding an important deal with the captioned company, we would like to know their financial standing and modes of business.

The reference they have given us is National Provincial Bank of London. Will you please approach the said bank for all possible information we require?

Any information you may furnish us will be treated strictly in confidence.

Sincerely yours,

[Signature]

Translate the Chinese given within the brackets in the following sentences.

1) We can assure you _____（你们给我们提供的任何情况）will be treated in absolute confidence.

2) Any information you may give us will be _____（将严格保密）.

3) Any information you can furnish as to their capital and reputation would be _____ _____（我们将非常重视并保密）.

4) _____（你方尽可放心）that any information you may provide will be treated as strictly confidential.

☞ **D. Read the following reply and see how it makes its comments on credit status.**

Dear Sirs,

In reply to your enquiry of November 21, Mr Muhmood Al-Roosan started in 2007 with a small capital. The business does not seem to have developed satisfactorily.

It appears that the capital is insufficient for the large stock carried and that he finds it difficult to obtain credit. Our advice is to supply on a cash basis only.

Please treat the information in strict confidence.

Yours sincerely,

[Signature]

Study the following examples.
- Making positive comments on one's credit and/or financial status
  * As far as we know, their financial standing is sound.
  * The firm you enquire about is one of the most reliable importers in our district and has for many years enjoyed a good reputation among the traders.
  * We believe that they owe their reputable position among the local wholesalers in our district to their steady and sincere way of conducting business.
  * At the moment, they are doing an active business. We may say that they are one of the several fast growing wholesale dealers in Accra handling laboratory and pharmaceutical equipment for their clients.
  * They are a firm of high reputation and have large financial reserves.
- Making negative comments on one's credit and/or financial status
  * In reply to your letter of June 21, we are sorry to say that our experience with the company which you enquire about has been unsatisfactory.
  * We are sorry to say that our experience with the company which you enquire about in your letter of June 21 has been unsatisfactory.
  * We are of the opinion that you would run into undue risk in granting them quarterly account terms.
  * It appears that the capital is insufficient for the large stock carried and that he finds it difficult to obtain credit.

E. Read the following letter and observe the expression used to give advice.

Dear Sirs,

Private & Confidential

After receiving your October 30 letter, we made enquiries respecting the firm you mentioned and have obtained the following information:

"Messrs. Willing & Co. made an arrangement with their creditors in December 2008. Their liabilities were £ 5,000, with assets £ 4,000. The creditors agreed to a composition of 60p in the pound. A first dividend of 20p was paid after six months and a second dividend of 20p three months later, but nothing further. The business is said to be making no progress at the present time, and we would advise you to exercise extreme caution in your dealings with this firm."

We have also made independent enquiries respecting the firm, and the result was a corroboration of our agent's report.

It would, therefore, appear inadvisable to enter into any credit transaction with these people.

You are welcome to this information free of charge, and we are pleased to have served you in the matter. But remember that this information is given in confidence and without any responsibility on our part.

Yours sincerely,
[Signature]

Complete the following sentences by using the words or expressions in the box.

> inadvisable   advise   exercise   suggest   caution

1) We have completed our enquiries concerning the firm mentioned in your letter of April 4 and regret that we must _____ you to regard their request for credit with caution.

2) We advise you to proceed with every possible _____ in dealing with the firm in question.

3) This is a case in which caution is necessary and we _____ that you make additional enquiries through an agency. We accept your assurance that the information we have given will be treated in strict confidence and regret that we cannot be more helpful.

4) It would, therefore, appear _____ to enter into any credit transaction with these people.

5) The business is said to be making no progress at the present time, and we would advise you to _____ extreme caution in your dealings with this firm.

3.3 Writers' Workshop: Businesslike Poise & Formal Style

Businesslike Poise and Formal Style for BE Letter Writing

Compared with private letters, BE letters are formal and serious of style. They are originated from the 19th century correspondence popular for foreign trade in Britain, which was well-known for its accounting or description of facts and "businesslike poise".

Traditionally, BE letters used to be very formal with the use of too many long and learned words, nominalisations, abused conventionalities and passive voice. All of these forms of language have become somewhat old-fashioned because they just sound dull and businesslike. In very formal situations such as asking to enter into business relations, credit enquiry, making claims and complaints about delayed shipment or payment, however, the language used can be very formal, showing many signs of what is known as "commercialese".

3.3.1 Group work

Work in groups of three or four to select the appropriate words or expressions and discuss the different effects for the use of learned and popular words or expressions in the following letter.

> Dear Sirs:
>
> *Would you kindly / Will you please* send us details of your bathroom fittings which you advertised in Business Week on October 11?
>
> *We would be grateful to you if you should / Please* quote us all the items listed in the enclosed inquiry form, giving your prices CIF Shanghai. *Would you kindly / Will you please* also indicate delivery time, your terms of payment and discount details for regular purchases and large orders?
>
> Our annual requirements for bathroom fittings are considerable, and we may be able to place substantial orders with you if your prices are competitive and your delivery is prompt.
>
> *Your quotation is expected by us / We are expecting your quotation.*
>
> Yours faithfully,
>
> Tom Zhang

3.3.2 Rewrite the following sentences, trying to make them not sound so businesslike or formal.

1) Your interest in our company is appreciated.
2) Please favour us with a prompt reply.
3) I should be grateful if you would be good enough to advise us when the shipment is to be effected.
4) Should you require any further clarification, please do not hesitate to contact the undersigned.
5) It is gratifying to learn from your letter of July 5 that you are interested in an offer from us for 20 metric tons of groundnuts for shipment to Odense.

3.3.3 Comment and improvement

Make your comment before you make any improvement.

> Dear Sirs,
>
> We have received your letter dated 27 March, 2021.
>
> We are extremely distressed to learn that an error was made pertaining to your esteemed order. Please be informed that the cause of your complaint has been investigated and it actually appears that the error occurred in our packing section and it was not discovered before this order was dispatched to your goodself.
>
> Arrangements have been made for a repeat order to be dispatched to you immediately and this should leave our warehouse later today. It is our sincere hope that you will have no cause for further complaint with replacement order.
>
> Once again we offer our humblest apologies for the unnecessary inconvenience that you have been

Unit 3 Credit Enquiries & Replies

caused in this instance.

Please find enclosed herewith a copy of new catalogue for your reference and perusal.

Kindly contact the undersigned if you require any further clarifications.

Very truly yours,

John Smith

Unit 4 Enquiries & Replies

Learning Objectives
- ✓ learning about how to make enquiries and replies
- ✓ learning how to make enquiries in writing
- ✓ learning how to reply to enquiries
- ✓ learning how to write openings and closings of letters

Identify Problems in the Following Writing & Comment

Dear Mr Smith,

    We have got your letter inquiring about our light-weight raincoats.

    As you may have found in the catalogue, we have got a dozen types of light-weight raincoats. For the quantities you mentioned, we are pleased to quote CIF Shanghai as follows: men's in small size, $ 2.75 for each other; men's in medium size, $ 3 for each other; women's in small size, $ 2.25 for each; and women's in medium size, $ 2.50 for each.

    Shipment will be effected within three to four weeks after we have received L/C.

    Looking forward to hearing from you soon.

Yours truly,
Thomas Hanson

4.1 Experience & Practice

4.1.1 Learning about how to make enquiries and replies to them

A. Brief introduction

Questions: *How do you think you should structure an enquiry? What are the differences between general enquiries and specific enquiries?*

① General Enquiries and Specific Enquiries

Business negotiation in international trade usually starts with an enquiry by an importer to an exporter, asking for the price list, catalogues, samples and details about the goods or trade terms and conditions. Sometimes, however, an exporter can also initiate the negotiation by making an enquiry to a foreign importer, including his intention of selling certain goods to the latter. It is worthy of note that whoever makes an enquiry he is not necessarily liable for the buying or the selling. And the receiver of an enquiry can choose to make no reply at all. But, according to the commercial practice the receiver of an enquiry will respond without delay in the usual form of a quotation, an offer, or a bid. To an old client, you may say how much you appreciate it. To a new customer, you may say that you are pleased to receive it and express your hope of building up a lasting friendly business relationship.

Generally, enquiries can be divided into two types: general enquiries and specific enquiries. In a general enquiry, the writer may ask only for catalogues, price lists or samples in order to get some general knowledge of the products in question. It is usually made after the set-up of business relations but before a specific enquiry. In a specific enquiry, the writer has a particular product in mind and wants the seller to provide more detailed information or make an offer for his product.

② Points to Remember
- In writing, enquiries and replies to them are usually written in a direct approach. In an enquiry and a reply to it, the customer or the supplier comes straight to the point right at the beginning, as is shown in the following letter (B.a). Thus it saves both the customer's and the supplier's precious time. But some enquiries may start with some necessary explanation or background information to show courtesy and respect, especially those written by new customers to suppliers.
- All in all, enquiries should be brief, specific, courteous and reasonable. In return, replies to enquiries should be prompt, courteous and helpful. In case the goods enquired for are currently out of stock, the supplier should inform the enquirer when they will be available and, by taking this opportunity, introduce some other products as substitutes so as to create a good impression, which hopefully will result in more business.

B. Experience by reading and answering questions.

a. Read the letter and answer the following questions.
- *Does the writer have any particular product in mind?*
- *How do you like the enquiry? General or specific?*

Dear Sir or Madam,

We're writing to enquire whether you have leather shoes available.

Will you please send us a copy of your catalogue and current price list for leather shoes? We are very interested in leather shoes for both men and children.

Our company, the leading shoes dealer in Shanghai, China, has branches in five neighboring cities. If the quality of your leather shoes is desirable and the prices are reasonable, we expect to place regular orders for fairly large numbers.

Will you please say whether, in these circumstances, you are able to allow us a special discount?

44 A Coursebook for Business English Writing

> This would enable us to maintain the low selling prices that have been an important reason for the growth of our business. In return, we would be prepared to place orders for a guaranteed annual minimum number of leather shoes, the figure to be mutually agreed.
>
>   Looking forward to your early reply.
>
>   Yours sincerely,
>   [Signature]

b. Read the reply to an enquiry and answer the following questions.
- *How is the reply? Is it courteous or not?*
- *What suggestion does the writer make? Why?*

☞ **C. Now read and comment on how the reply is made.**

> Gentlemen,
>   We warmly welcome your enquiry of March 17 and thank you for your interest in our cotton piece goods.
>   We are enclosing our illustrated catalogue and price list giving the details you asked for. As for the payment terms we usually require confirmed, irrevocable Letter of Credit payable by draft at sight.
>   We have already sold some of these products to the United States. May we suggest that you contact the Textiles Export Ltd. in New York directly? We think the firm may supply you with more details of our cotton piece goods. We feel confident that you will find the goods are both excellent in quality and very reasonable in price.
>
>   Sincerely yours,
>   [Signature]

4.1.2 Practice

☞ **A. Read the following telephone conversation and then on Mr Clive's behalf, write a letter on its basis.**

Mr Clive: I'm glad to have the opportunity of visiting your stand. I hope we can do business together.

Mr Wang: It's a great pleasure to meet you, Mr Clive. I believe you have seen our exhibits in the show room. What is it in particular you're interested in?

Mr Clive: I'm interested in your low wattage Microwave Ovens. I've seen the exhibits and studied your catalogues. I think some of the items will find a ready market in Canada. Here's a list of requirements, I'd like to have your lowest quotations, CIF Vancouver.

Mr Wang: Thank you for your enquiry. Would you tell us what quantity you require so that we can work out the offers?

Mr Clive: I'll do that. Meanwhile, would you please give me an indication of the price?

Mr Wang: Here is our FOB price. All the prices in the lists are subject to our confirmation.

☞ **B. Now you have received the following letter enquiring about the electric fans you are dealing in.**

Dear Sir or Madam,

Re: Electric Fan

We are one of the leading importers of electric goods in this city and shall be pleased to establish business relations with your corporation.

Now we are interested in your electric fans, details as per our Enquiry Note 1345 attached, and shall be pleased to receive your lowest quotation as soon as possible.

If your price is attractive and delivery date acceptable, we shall place our order with you immediately.

Yours faithfully,
[Signature]

Write a reply according to the following requirements:

- Express your thanks for receiving the incoming letter and also your pleasure in knowing the addressee's interest in entering into business relations with you.
- Tell that your fans are good quality and the price is competitive.
- Tell that delivery can be made in two months when the order is received.
- Say that you are expecting the addressee's order.

4.1.3 Case study & practice

Imagine that you are manager of the purchasing department of a trading company in China. You saw an advertisement posted on the Internet and want to import the chemical products made in SK Group. Write a letter enquiring about their chemical products.

In the East, it's one of the best known companies.
In the West, it's one of the best kept secrets.

SK Group—the perfect partner for your business

SK Group is one of Korea's leading businesses with annual sales of more than 12 billion. We produce a wide range of products, from oil, chemicals and plastics to fibres, textiles and magnetic media. We sell over 2,000 products in 36 countries.

In the United States alone, we have a turnover of $1 billion annually. If you are looking for a perfect partner for business, please contact:

SK Group
36-1 2-Ga Ulchiro, Chung-Gu
Seoul 100−192, Republic of Korea

Tel +8227582114
Fax +8227549414
Visit our website at: www.sk.com.kr

4.2 Communicating & Writing Skills

☞ **A. Read and learn how to make requests in writing.**

Dear Sirs,

We are pleased to learn from our associates that you are one of the leading exporters of garments in China. There is a steady market here for silk garments of high quality. We are engaged in garment business for many years, and we are sure that Chinese silk garments will sell very well in this country.

Please send us a copy of your catalogue and the latest price list for silk garments for both men and women. It would also be helpful if you could send us a sample-cutting book.

If you can supply high quality silk garments at competitive prices, we may place regular orders for large quantities. In the circumstances, please indicate whether you will allow us a special discount and tell us the details of your payment and delivery terms.

We are looking forward to your early reply.

Yours faithfully,

[Signature]

Change the underlined words of the following sentences with the expressions given below.

| we should thank you for | it is found necessary for you | Please |
| We would be grateful | Could you please | |

1) <u>Could you please</u> confirm that your prices are the same?
2) <u>I would appreciate it</u> if you could recommend a good hotel to me.
3) We are, at present, very much interested in importing your chinaware and <u>we would appreciate</u> your sending us catalogues, sample books or even samples if possible.
4) <u>Would you please</u> send us your CV so that we could review your experience?
5) In the meantime, <u>you are requested</u> to furnish us with the name of your bank prior to the conclusion of the first transaction between us.

B. Read and learn how to make brief explanation in writing.

Dear Sirs,

We have recently received a number of requests for your Giant bicycles of the current model and have good reasons to believe that we could place regular orders with you if your prices are competitive. Would you please quote us FOB Vancouver for 1,000 sets of men's Giant bicycles and inform the earliest date of shipment?

There is a large demand for bicycles in our country, where cycling is becoming popular. Owing to the high price of petrol, it is likely that more and more people will use bicycles of high quality and fashionable design like yours.

We shall be pleased to do business with you, and we would appreciate it if you could give us a favourable quotation.

We look forward to hearing from you soon.

Yours faithfully,
[Signature]

Rewrite the underlined words of the following sentences by using the words or expressions given in the box.

| favourable | enquiries | are convinced that | main | put | enter into |

1) We have recently received a number of <u>requests</u> for your Giant bicycles of the current model and <u>have good reasons to believe that</u> we could place regular orders with you if your prices are <u>competitive</u>.
2) We saw your advertisement <u>posted</u> on the Internet on March 10 about your textile products. At present we are interested in pure cotton bed-sheets.
3) We are one of the <u>leading</u> importers of electric goods in this city and shall be pleased to <u>establish</u> business relations with your corporation.

C. Read and learn how to make enquiries in writing.

Dear Sirs,

We are interested in obtaining catalogues and price lists of your embroidered linen products. In particular, we are interested in table linens of various types, such as tablecloths, napkins, and towels.

Our company, a diversified international business house, is just about to start a new marketing and distribution system in America with embroidered linen products, particularly with customer designed products. To develop this business, we need to know the following items of information:

1. Is it possible to order custom-made goods with our customer logo or name?
2. What is the minimum number of pieces for such an order?

3. How can we see the quality of your products? Can you send us some samples of different designs? If we have to purchase the samples, please let us know of it before you send them to us.

Please also let us know of any questions you may have about this project or our company.

Thank you for your cooperation in this matter. We greatly appreciate your help in providing answers to our enquiries.

Yours sincerely,
[Signature]

Translate the following Chinese into English.

1) We visited your stand at the Canton Fair and are now writing you to _____ _____（询问有关丝制领带的情况）.

2) Please tell if you can offer this product and include _____ （订货至交货所需时间、包装和中国离岸价）.

3) Please tell us _____（最高现金折扣和最早交货时间）.

4) Would you please _____（报新家具的交货和安装价）for the refectory and office areas of our company?

5) We are thinking of getting a supply of quilts. Please send us your best offer by fax _____（说明产地和包装）.

6) The illustrations will also _____（向你们介绍）about other casual shoes we are exporting.

☞ **D. Read and learn how to give tactful reminders.**

Dear Sir,

We learn with pleasure from your letter of May 26 that you have a variety of new MP4 players in stock. We are interested in your 1.5 inch color LCD MP4 player in the "Super Memory" Range.

Please send us the catalogue and price list and all necessary information so as to acquaint us with the detailed description of technological specifications.

Meanwhile, please quote us the lowest price CIF Seattle, stating the earliest date of shipment.

We are an established and also experienced online store selling electronic products in the USA. We have a large number of regular customers. If you can offer us competitive prices and the delivery time is acceptable, we shall place a large order with you.

We trust you will send us a prompt reply.

Yours truly,
[Signature]

Translate the following Chinese into English.

1) _____（如果条件和交货时间令人满意的话）, we should expect to place regular orders with you.

2) _____（如果价格优惠、交货日期可行）, we intend to place a large order with you.

3) _____（如果你方所报价格优惠的话）, there will be broad prospects for your pure cotton bed sheets.

E. Read and observe the expression used to express the writer's pleasure in providing something.

Dear Sirs,

Many thanks for your enquiry and we are very pleased to know that you have interest in our embroidered linen products.

To give you a general idea of the products we deal in, we are pleased to send you our latest catalogue and price list as well as a sample book that you ask for in your letter. And the minimum number you order for custom-made goods with customer logo or name is usually 20,000 pieces.

If you need any more information, please let us know. And we are sure that our cooperation will be successful and profitable.

We look forward to receiving your first order.

Sincerely yours,
[Signature]

Complete the following sentences by using the expressions given below.

| We are pleased to | We have pleasure | We are appreciative |
| We are pleased | It gives us pleasure to | |

1) _____ send you the catalogues asked for in your letter of April 20.

2) _____ send you patterns for grey flannels which we can supply from stock.

3) _____ in enclosing three copies of our illustrated catalogue and price list of the shoes that we produce.

4) _____ of your effort to put our new products on your market and hope the information enclosed herewith will be of great help to you.

5) _____ to forward you the samples of our products with their quotations and discounts for your reference.

50 A Coursebook for Business English Writing

☞ **F. Read and observe the expression used to express the writer's regret in inability to provide something.**

> Dear Sir/Madam,
> 　　We were happy to receive your enquiry of October 12 concerning the supply of black silk.
> 　　Unfortunately, there has been a heavy demand for the above since last year, we are consequently fully committed at the moment and are unable to supply the goods as requested.
> 　　We assure you, however, that we shall fax you as soon as fresh supplies become available. Should your customers require other silks, please let us know.
> 　　Thank you again for your enquiry. We hope we will be able to serve you again.
> 　　　　　　　　　　　　　　　　　　　　　　　　　　Yours sincerely,
> 　　　　　　　　　　　　　　　　　　　　　　　　　　Bruce Williamson

Complete the following sentences by translating the expressions in brackets into English.

1) _____（令人遗憾的是）we cannot make delivery within 2 months from receipt of your order, owing to a heavy demand for the article from Canada.
2) _____（很遗憾地告诉你们）that we do not have in stock the goods of the desired quality.
3) _____（很遗憾）that it is impossible to accept your counter offer, even to meet you halfway for the price of raw material has risen 20%.
4) Although we are anxious to open up business with you, _____ _____（很遗憾,我们不可能按你们的要求减价）.
5) We are sorry to tell you that _____（我们不能满足你方需求）for the said goods now. When our supplies are replenished next month, we shall arrange to manufacture the goods immediately and fill our order in the last ten days of next month.

☞ **G. Read and observe the expression used to promote sales.**

> Dear Sirs,
> 　　Thank you for your enquiry of May 14 and for your interest in our hand-made artificial leather gloves. We are enclosing our illustrated catalogue and price-list giving the details you ask for. Also under separate cover we are sending you a full range of samples and, when you examine them, you will agree that the goods are both excellent in quality and very reasonable in price.
> 　　On regular purchase in quantities, of not less than five gross of individual items we would allow you a trade discount of 30%.
> 　　We also export a wide range of hand-made leather shoes in which you may be interested. They are fully illustrated in the catalogue and are of the same high quality as our gloves.

> We are sure that the samples will reach you in good time and look forward to your order.
>
> Yours faithfully,
>
> [Signature]

Translate the following expressions in the brackets into English.

1) From the attached price list you can see that _____ (我们设法压低报价) though prices have gone up steadily since October. We hope that you will let us have your order before further rises in costs make increases unavoidable.

2) Our products, especially our cameras, _____ (在西欧国家深受欢迎). Because of their excellent quality and low prices, you can be sure our products will no doubt help you expand our market.

3) _____ (我们的产品将在贵国畅销).

4) Our goods will _____ (前景看好).

5) As the goods of your specifications are in short supply, we intend to furnish you with our T-315 _____ (作为替代品), which is of good quality and _____ (十分接近你们的规格要求) but will be offered at a more favorable price.

6) The illustrations will also _____ (向你们介绍) about other casual shoes we are exporting.

4.3　Writers' Workshop: Opening & Closing a Letter

Opening a Letter

How to begin a letter depends. At the beginning of a letter, you may choose to state the aim(s) or objective(s) directly by referring to the topic in a simple sentence. The most frequently-used expression is the infinitive phrase as is seen in the sentence:

- *I am writing to confirm the details of our conversation last week, concerning our enquiry about your TV sets.*

Or you may choose to start with a brief self-introduction and an expression of your intention for writing the letter, as is shown in the following example:

- *We are one of the leading importers of textiles in Russia and shall be pleased to establish direct trade relations with you.*

If you are answering a letter, however, you can start like this:

- *Thank you for your letter of ... (date) asking if ... or enquiring about ...*
- *We have received your letter of ... (date) concerning ...*

Closing a Letter

The most common way to end or close a letter might be the use of the expressions that are given below:

- I look forward to receiving your reply/order.
- Looking forward to hearing from you.

Just like the beginning of a letter, the closing of a letter also depends. If you give some information in the letter, you can close a letter like this:

- I hope that this information will help you.
- Please contact me / let me know if you need any further information.
- Please feel free to contact me if you have any further questions.

4.3.1 Group work

Work in groups of 3 or 4 and try to write in the following situations.

1) You have seen a job advertised in the January 7 *Shanghai Morning Post*. Write to apply to them for the job of Junior Accounts Clerk.
2) You want to know the prices of some TV sets.
3) You have been asked to offer 10% reduction on the price of the holidays to Mexico. Say "yes" to the request at the beginning of your reply.
4) A company wrote to you on July 23. They wanted to know whether you sell computers.
5) Tell the addressee that he is welcome to contact you if he needs any further information.

4.3.2 Choosing the correct opening or closing from the sentences to complete the letters

1) Please feel free to contact me if you need any information about our other branches.
2) Thank you for your letter of April 3 in which you asked us to send you details of the ladies' and children's shoes that we manufacture in leather and P.V.C.
3) Please write to us when you require further information, which shall always have our best attention.
4) Thank you so much for asking me to participate in the Community Pageant.

Dear Sirs,

_____

_____

Here we enclose three copies of our illustrated catalogue and price list of the shoes that we produce. From these you will be able to see that we can offer a very wide range of shoes and that the styles are modern and very popular. Under separate cover we are also sending you a sample pair of ladies' shoes in leather and a children's pair in P.V.C. You will see from these that the quality is very high and the material used will stand up to poor weather conditions.

Looking forward to your first order.

Yours sincerely,
[Signature]

②

Dear Peter,

Thank you for your telephone call today.

I am sorry that I was not in the office when you rang, but here is the information that you wanted. The address of our branch in Singapore is 54 Liu Fang Road, Jurong Town, Singapore 2262. The manager is Mr S Rushford.

                                            Yours sincerely,
                                            John Blake

③

Dear Mr Bryant,

How I wish that I could join you, but unfortunately, my monthly trip to the West Coast is scheduled for the week of the pageant.

Although I'm disappointed that I can't accept your thoughtful invitation, I wish you much success in arranging this year's festivities.

                                            With best wishes,
                                            [Signature]

④

Dear Sir,

Thanks for your letter of January 17, asking us for details and prices of our electric heaters. Enclosed please find our latest price list and catalogue, together with Model X-4's details.

                                            Yours faithfully,
                                            John Smith
                                            Electrical Appliances Co., Ltd.

4.3.3　Comment & improvement

Read the following letter and comment on its opening before you make any improvement.

Dear Sirs,

After a thorough investigation, we did not find any error on our side because we took great care to execute your order as shown in the enclosed certificate of packing inspection. Moreover, the lots were on board the ship in perfect condition which was clearly stated in the clean B/L.

Therefore, we suggest that you lodge a claim with the insurance company. We will assist you wherever possible to process the claim.

Thank you for writing to us about the quality of the air switches covering your order No. 5678.

                                            Yours sincerely,
                                            [Signature]

Unit 5 Quotations, Offers & Counter-offers

Learning Objectives

- ✓ learning about how to make quotations, offers and counter-offers
- ✓ learning how to make quotations, offers and counter-offers
- ✓ learning how to perform relative functions of language and communication
- ✓ learning how to make proposition and counter-proposition in BE writing

---

Identify Problems in the Following Writing & Comment

Gentlemen,

　　We are quite sure that you will be interested in hearing about our company, which specializes in stunning interior design projects for people who have a bit of money. Our philosophy is that only the best is good enough for our clients, but then many of our customers are household names, so they're not exactly poor.

　　We're not afraid of using the best, and most expensive materials because we know we can pass the cost on to you.

　　If you want a color brochure, and if you feel that you can afford the kind of prices we charge, fill in this form and we'll send you one.

Yours sincerely,
[Signature]

5.1　Experience & Practice

5.1.1　Learning about how to make quotations, offers and counter-offers

☞ **A. Brief introduction**

Questions: *What is a quotation, offer and counter-offer? And what is to be included in a quotation or an offer?*

① Quotation, Offer and Counter-offer

　　Making a quotation or an offer is a most important step or the first step in negotiating an export transaction.

　　A quotation is a promise to supply goods on the terms agreed upon by both sides. But it can not be seen as an offer because it just includes a notice of the price of certain goods being sold. It is not an offer in the legal sense because the seller can withdraw it and the prospective buyer is not obliged to purchase the goods for which a quotation is requested.

An offer refers to a promise to supply goods on the terms and conditions in which the seller not only quotes the terms of price but also indicates all necessary terms of sales for the buyer's consideration and acceptance. In addition, an offer may be classified into a firm offer, i.e. an offer at a stated price within a certain time limit; and a non-firm offer, i.e. an offer made without engagement. In the latter case it is subject to confirmation by the seller after being accepted by the buyer.

When an offeree receives the offer, he may show disagreement to some terms such as price or payment terms in the offer; he may even make a counter-offer, i.e. virtually a partial rejection of the original offer stating his own terms instead. Then the original offerer or seller becomes the offeree. If he also disagrees with the relative terms in the counter-offer, he may send a counter-offer to the buyer. So a deal is usually concluded only after several cycles or rounds of bargaining. In other words, very often, it is only after the exchange of a number of letters by means of e-mails and/or faxes that the two parties come entirely to terms. In such a case the buyer, when finally placing his formal order, would accept the terms and conditions agreed upon for the seller's confirmation, which will be followed by the signature of the relative Sales Confirmation or Contract.

② Points to Remember

In general, a quotation or an offer includes:
- Description of the quality and quantity of the goods enquired about;
- Prices of the goods required (Make clear whether or not the quoted prices are to include delivery, for failure to do this may lead to subsequent disagreement with the buyer.);
- Terms of payment;
- Date of delivery;
- Period of validity, etc.

B. Experience by reading and answering questions.

① Read the quotation letter and answer the following questions.
- *How do you like the quotation? Is it a general quotation or specific?*
- *Does the writer of the letter make any request for a favorable price?*

Dear Sirs,

　　Thank you for your letter dated August 25. We are pleased to know that you are producing different kinds of shoes.

　　We are interested in your various casual shoes recommended in your letter particularly embroidered slippers and cotton shoes. Will you kindly send us a copy of your illustrated catalogue and some samples with further information? We shall be obliged if you could also quote your lowest prices CIF Liverpool, stating earliest date of shipment.

> Casual shoes of high quality are popular. We believe there is a promising market in our area for moderately priced goods of the types mentioned. If your price is competitive, we will consider placing an order for 5,000 pairs with you. We are looking forward to your urgent reply.
>
> Yours faithfully,
> [Signature]

b. Read the quotation letter and answer the following questions.

- *How do you like the quotation? Are the terms of trade complete?*
- *How is the presentation of the letter?*

⊕ **Quotation for stationery**

> Dear Sir,
>
> In reply to your enquiry of yesterday, we are pleased to make our quotation as listed below:
>
> 1. 10 doz.   Ball pens (Black)   @ US $10.00 per doz.
> 2. 5 doz.   Pencils (Red)   @ US $5.00 per doz.
> 3. 5 doz.   Erasers   @ US $12.00 per doz.
> 4. 5 doz.   Sharpeners   @ US $9.00 per doz.
> 5. 5 doz.   Ball pens (Blue)   @ US $4.00 per doz.
> 6. 10 doz.   Exercise books   @ US $15.00 per doz.
>
> Samples of the goods can be inspected at our above address, or we can send our representative to your office with samples for your inspection at our expense.
>
> The rates quoted above are net. We can make delivery of the goods at your office as desired at our expense. And we accept payment of the bills in two months' time from the date of delivery of goods.
>
> We look forward to receiving your order, and meanwhile enclose a copy of our catalogue in which you will find details of our other products. If you have any queries, please let us know.
>
> Yours sincerely,
> [Signature]

c. Read the reply to the above quotation and answer the following questions.

- *Does the writer accept the quotation? How do you know that?*
- *What expectation does the writer make in the closing?*

> Dear Sirs,
>
> Thank you for your letter of June 11 offering us your stationery. We find you have a good assortment of stationery and we are satisfied with the samples you sent to our office for our inspection. So we are pleased to place a trial order with you for the following:
>
> 1. 100 doz.   Ball pens (Black)   @ US $10.00 per doz.
> 2. 500 doz.   Pencils (Red)   @ US $5.00 per doz.
> 3. 500 doz.   Erasers   @ US $12.00 per doz.
> 4. 500 doz.   Sharpeners   @ US $9.00 per doz.
> 5. 500 doz.   Ball pens (Blue)   @ US $4.00 per doz.
> 6. 1,000 doz.   Exercise books   @ US $15.00 per doz.

The other terms are as follows:

The above prices are net and inclusive of the delivery of goods at our office at your expense.

The payment of the bills is made in two months' time from the date of delivery of goods.

We should appreciate your prompt delivery of the goods to our office and hope to enter into a lasting business relationship if this trial order proves to be satisfactory.

Yours sincerely,

d. Read the reply to the counter-offer and answer the following questions.
- *Why is the letter a counter-offer?*
- *What does the writer ask for? What does the proforma invoice function as?*

Dear Sirs,

Thank you for your sample. If you can accept US $4.50 per set FOB Shanghai, please send us your proforma invoice and we shall be ready to place an order for 500 sets of SM-468. There is no question about our getting the necessary import license from our authorities. After the said license is approved, we shall establish an irrevocable letter of credit in your favour.

Your prompt attention to this matter will be appreciated.

Yours faithfully,

5.1.2 Practice

A. Read the following conversation at the Guangzhou Trade Fair and then on Mr Wang's behalf, make an offer on its basis.

Mr Smith: I'm here at the Guangzhou Fair to do some market survey, obtain some samples and, if possible, place some orders.

Mr Wang: We have some samples in our showroom. Would you like to have a look first?

Mr Smith: Yes, I'd like to. As a matter of fact, I'm primarily interested in canned pear.

Mr Wang: As you know, our company has been exporting a lot of canned pear. They are right over there.

Mr Smith: They look very good. I'm especially interested in Art. No. 3 and No. 4. Can you quote on them?

Mr Wang: Certainly. I have the price list here for all of our articles quoted FOB Guangzhou.

Mr Smith: Can you quote a CIF price for me?

Mr Wang: Certainly. Let me figure it out. Yes, here it is!

Mr Smith: Thanks. Is your offer a firm one or subject to your final confirmation?

Mr Wang: A firm one, which remains open for 3 days.

Mr Smith: If my order is for a larger quantity, say, 50 metric tons, could you give us some discount?
Mr Wang: In that case, we are prepared to reduce our price by 3 percent.
Mr Smith: That's good. But can't you extend the offer for a few more days? I'll call home to have it discussed.
Mr Wang: What about two more days?
Mr Smith: That's fine. With this extension, I think the transaction will be put through.
Mr Wang: I hope so.

B. **Read the offer in the following and make your comment. Then write a reply, making a counter-offer asking for 2% reduction in the price.**

Dear Mr Boswell,

Re: Chinese Printed Shirting

Thank you for your letter of February 15 and we are glad to note that there are very brisk demands for the captioned goods in your city.

We are pleased to make you the following special offer, subject to our final confirmation:

Art. No. 83416 Printed Shirting
Design No. 77612-3B
Specifications: 30×36
Quantity: 20,000 metres
Packing: In bales or in wooden cases, at your option
Price: US $4 per metre CIF New York
Shipment: To be made in three equal monthly installments, beginning from Dec., 2008
Payment: By confirmed, irrevocable L/C payable by draft at sight to be opened 30 days before the time of shipment.

We have made a goods selection of samples suited to your country, and send them to you today by parcel post. Their fine quality, attractive designs and the reasonable prices will convince you that these goods are of good value.

We are expecting to receive your order.

Yours truly,
Liming Tang

5.1.3 Case study & practice

Read the following firm offer and complete it according to the Chinese given in the brackets. Then write a reply accepting the offer.

Dear Sirs,

Subj: "White Rabbit" Woolen Blanket

Thank you for your letter of March 20, in which you express your interest in our woolen blanket.

At your request, we are pleased to make you an offer, _____① _____ (直到 3 月 26 日前有

效), as follows:
   Commodity: "White Rabbit" Brand Woolen Blanket No. 45
   Size: 72×84 in. (182×213cm.)
   Colour: Yellow
   Quantity: 200 pcs
   Price: US $40 each piece CIF Montreal
   Shipment: During August/ September
   Payment: By 100% confirmed, irrevocable Letter of Credit in our favor payable by draft at sight to reach the Sellers one month before shipment and remain valid for negotiation in China till the 15th day after shipment.

   As you may have realized from the catalogue we sent you in January, our blanket is a perfect combination of warmth, softness, and easy care. We are confident that ＿＿＿＿＿＿＿＿＿ ②＿＿＿＿＿ ＿＿＿＿＿(贵方将有利可图).
   We look forward to your prompt reply.

                                                    Yours faithfully,
                                                    [Signature]

5.2 Communicating & Writing Skills

☞ **A. Compare the following two letters and learn how to make a quotation and also how to make an offer.**

⊕ **Quotation for asphalt**

Dear Sirs,
   In reply to your letter of 21st November, we have enclosed a detailed asphalt quotation. Besides those advertised in the *Builders' Journal*, our illustrated catalogue also enclosed shows various varieties of asphalt. Most types can be supplied from stock. 45–60 days should be allowed for delivery of those marked with an asterisk.
   Building contractors in Hong Kong and Taiwan have found our petroleum asphalt are superior in quality. And our quotation is the most affordable. We can allow a discount of 2% on all orders of US $6,000 value and over, and 3% on orders of more than US $20,000. Any orders you place with us will be processed promptly.
   Thank you for your letter again and looking forward to your reply.

                                                    Yours sincerely,
                                                    [Signature]

⊕ **Offer made at the importer's request**

Dear Mr Smith,
                                    Re: Groundnuts
   Thank you for your letter of July 5 and we are glad to learn that you are interested in an offer from us for 20 metric tons of groundnuts for shipment to Odense.

We are making you, subject to your acceptance reaching us not later than July 30 the following offer:

"20 metric tons of Shandong Groundnuts, Handpicked and Ungraded at RMB ¥800 per metric ton CIF Odense for shipment during October/November, 2021. Other terms and conditions same as usual."

As no direct steamer is available from here to Odense, the goods will have to be transshipped at Copenhagen. Please note that the additional cost from Copenhagen to Odense is included in the quoted price.

For your information, there has been lately a large demand for groundnuts and such a growing demand can only result in increased price. However, you may profit by this advancing market if you let us have our acceptance immediately.

Yours sincerely,
William London

Substitute the underlined expressions with those given in the box below.

| make you the following offer | send you our quotation | make you an offer for |
| it is our pleasure | it is gratifying for us | |

1) Thank you for your enquiry of October 24 and we are pleased to <u>make you the following quotation</u>.
2) Thank you for your recent fax telling us that there is a good demand for our "Panda" televisions in your market. We are pleased to <u>offer them as follows</u>.
3) Thank you for your enquiry of December 20 and we can <u>offer you</u> the soybeans you required. This offer will remain open until the receipt of your fax by return.
4) Thank you for your March 3 letter enquiring for our sewing machines and <u>we are pleased</u> to fax you an offer as follows:...
5) Thank you for your letter of January 19. And <u>we are pleased</u> to make the following offer, subject to our final confirmation.

B. Compare the following two letters and learn how to make a firm and a non-firm offer.

⊕ **A letter making a non-firm offer of jute**

Dear Sir,

Re: Offering 5,000 Long Tons Jute

Thank you for your letter of August 15. At your request, we offer:
(1) Name of Commodity: Bangladesh Jute, 2008 crop
(2) Quantity: 5,000 long tons (shipping weight)

(3) Quality and Specifications: First grade. Quality should not be lower than the established standard of our Jute Board. Moisture regain should not be more than 19.04%.

(4) Unit Price: US $450 per long ton CIF Guangzhou

(5) Time of Shipment: No later than October 20, 2008 in one lot

(6) Terms of Payment: By confirmed, irrevocable, transferable and divisible L/C by draft at sight

The above offer is subject to our final confirmation. Please reply by fax immediately.

Yours faithfully,

[Signature]

⊕ A letter making a firm offer of Chinese embroidered silk table cloths

Dear Sirs,

Thank you for your letter of January 22 enquiring about our embroidered silk table cloths. At your request, we are making you a firm offer, subject to your reply reaching us before February 22, as follows:

Commodity: Chinese Embroidered Silk Table Cloths

Size: 150mm×150mm

Quantity: Forty thousand (40,000) pieces

Packing: 2 bales of 20 pieces, to a carton

Price: US $250.00 (Two hundred and fifty US dollars) per piece, FOB Ningbo

Payment: By confirmed, irrevocable L/C payable at sight in our favour

Shipment: Within 30 days after receipt of your L/C

As you know, there is a good market for Chinese Embroidered Silk Table Cloths and the price still keeps going up at present. Besides, in order to enable us to effect early shipment, we expect the relevant L/C is opened in time.

We look forward to your immediate reply.

Yours sincerely,

[Signature]

Study the following examples.

- Stipulating the condition for validity of a non-firm offer

a) The prices are subject to our final confirmation by fax.

b) The prices are valid only if the current prices of raw materials do not change.

c) Thank you for your enquiry and we are pleased to make you the following offer, subject to prior sale.

d) The above offer is valid, subject to goods being unsold.

e) The prices are subject to change without notice.

- Setting forth the validity of a firm offer

a) Our prices are binding until November 10.

b) Our prices are in force only if you order by return mail.

c) This offer remains effective (valid, firm, open) for ten days from January 15.

d) At your request, we now hold this offer firm (open) till January 15.

e) At your request, we now keep this firm offer open for a further ten days from January 15.

☞ **C. Read and learn how to bargain in a counter-offer.**

> Dear Duncan,
>
> <u>Re: Canned Fish</u>
>
> Thank you for your offer by fax of October 5 for 5,000 pieces of the captioned goods at £ 3.50 per piece CIF Hamburg.
>
> Regretfully, our end-users here find your price too high and out of line with the prevailing market price. Information indicates that some European goods have been sold at the level of £ 3.20 per piece.
>
> Your reduction of price would make it easier for us to persuade our end-users to accept your price, as goods of similar quality is easily obtainable at a much lower figure. If you could reduce your limit by, say, 10%, we might come to terms.
>
> It is in view of our long-standing business relationship that we make you such a counter-offer. As the market is falling, we hope you will consider our counter-offer and fax us your acceptance as soon as possible.
>
> We expect your early reply.
>
> Sincerely yours,
>
> John Housman

Complete the following sentences by translating the expressions in the brackets.

1) Upon checking your offer, we would like to say that your price seems _____(比我们料想的高了一点).

2) We find your prices _____(与现行市场价格不符).

3) We could send large orders if you could reduce your price to _____ (与你们竞争者的价格可比的水平)in this market.

4) We regret to say that we cannot accept your offer because _____ (你们的价格相当高).

5) We are obliged to place our order elsewhere unless you manage to reduce your prices to _____(经得起竞争).

☞ **D. Read the following letter and observe how to make a conditional concession.**

> Dear Sirs,
>
> We are sorry to hear that you think our last offer for the above is too high.
>
> After careful rechecking, we would specially reduce 5% for the order quantity of 40,000 sets to show our sincerity.
>
> As you know, NTD to USD has been appreciated for more than 10%, the price we reoffered above is already our cost.
>
> Please take the above into consideration and decide your order soon.
>
> Sincerely yours,
>
> [Signature]

Complete the following sentences by using the expressions below.

> the long connection between us in this line of business
> your minimum quantity for the first order reaches 300 dozens
> help you develop business
> a considerable increase of your orders

1) We hope that this concession will lead to _____.
2) However, in order to _____, we are prepared to allow you a special discount of 3% on an order amounting to 500,000 pcs or over.
3) We may consider allowing you a 3% commission if _____.
4) However, in view of _____, we have decided to reduce the price by 10%, which is the furthest we can go to help you.

☞ **E. Read the following letter and observe how to say what one can do and cannot do.**

Dear Sir,

Thank you for your letter of May 24. Your comments on our offer of socks have drawn our close attention.

Although we are keen to meet your requirements, we very much regret that we are unable to comply with your request to reduce the price as our prices are closely calculated. Even if there is a slight difference between our prices and those of our other suppliers, you will find it profitable to buy from us because the quality of our products is superior to that of other foreign makers available in your district.

However, we desire to develop business with you. In order to help you to push the sale of our products, we are prepared to allow you a 5% discount provided your order calls for a minimum quantity of 8,000 pairs.

If the proposal is acceptable to you, please let us have your order at an early date.

Yours sincerely,
Tom Brown

Write something in the following situations.

1) The buyer asks to quote him on FOB basis, but you usually do business on CIF terms.
2) Say that you cannot grant the reduction asked for as your price is moderately fixed.
3) Say that you cannot accept the buyer's counter-offer as it leaves you with little profit.
4) Say that you cannot accept the buyer's counter-offer or even meet him halfway. And say that the best you can do is to reduce your previous quotation by 2%.

A Coursebook for Business English Writing

F. Rearrange the following sentences.

Dear Sirs,

<u>A Firm Offer for Tin Foil Sheets</u>

① You will note from our fax that we can offer you 50 long tons of Tin Foil Sheets at the attractive price of Stg. 135 per long ton CFR Shanghai for delivery within one month after your placing an order with us.

② Payment of the purchase is to be effected by an irrevocable letter of credit in our favor, payable by draft at sight in Pounds Sterling in London.

③ Thank you for your letter of March 15 and we confirm having faxed you today in reply.

④ The goods cannot remain unsold once this particular offer has lapsed.

⑤ This offer is firm subject to your immediate reply reaching us here not later than the end of this month.

Yours sincerely,

[Signature]

5.3 Writers' Workshop: Proposition vs Counter-proposition

Proposition vs Counter-proposition in Writing Offers & Counter-offers

It is very common to make proposition and counter-proposition in business. People often make propositions of acquiring another enterprise, but they are often rejected. This writing approach of proposition and counter-proposition is, however, often taken to make offers and counter-offers in trade negotiation. As is known to all, a deal is usually concluded after a cycle of offer and counter-offer and counter counter-offer. When a proposition is made, it is usually followed by supporting facts or reasons. When you accept the proposition, you can simply say "yes". If you disagree to the proposition, you will say "no" or make a counter-proposition by giving your own reasons to support it.

5.3.1 Group work

Work in groups and try to write in the following situations by using the following verbs.

| regret | let's | offer | on the high side |

1) The price gap is too wide to be filled. Say that the largest cut you can allow is 4%.
2) Make a suggestion that you meet each other half way.
3) Tell the seller that his price is high.
4) You have had to raise your prices because the government has increased the sales tax.

5.3.2 Reading the following letter and analysing how it develops textually

Dear Sirs,

Thank you for your letter of June 6, offering us the captioned goods at US $20 per dozen CIF London.

In reply, we very much regret to say that your price is rather high and out of line with the prevailing market level.

Information indicates that some parcels of Japanese make have been sold at the level of US $16.5 per dozen. So if you should reduce your price by, say, 5%, we might come to terms.

Because of our long-standing business relationship, we make you such a counter-offer. As the market is declining, we sincerely hope you will consider our counter-offer and fax us soon.

Yours sincerely,

John Smith

5.3.3 Comment and improvement

Comment on the following adjustment letter and improve it.

Dear Mr. Peterson,

In your September 19 claim of wireless phone in your model HW586, you said that you have had the phone for 15 months, which is well beyond our one-year guarantee. Even though your repair person says that you had problems earlier, he is not one of our authorized repair people. If you will read the warranty carefully, you will see that we honor the warranty only when our authorized repair people find defects. I think you will understand why we must follow this procedure.

After considering the information received, we regret to report that we cannot reimburse you for the purchase. But I am confident that if you take the phone to the authorized service center in your area, they can correct the defect at reasonable charge. If I can be of additional service, please contact me.

Sincerely yours,

May Philips

# Unit 6 Orders & Replies

Learning Objectives

✓ learning about how to place orders and make replies
✓ learning how to place orders and make replies
✓ learning how to perform relative functions of language and communication
✓ learning how to write in inductive or in deductive pattern of organisation

---

Identify Problems in the Following Writing & Comment

Dear Mr Chen,

    We have got your letter of July 12 and received patterns of your cotton prints. We'd like to order the following items:

Quantity	Pattern No.	Prices
400 meters	28	$ 200 per meter
500 meters	48	$ 150 per meter
300 meters	69	$ 120 per meter

We are looking forward to your reply.

                    Sincerely yours,
                    Mary Smith

6.1 Experience & Practice

6.1.1 Learning about how to place orders and make replies

☞ **A. Brief introduction**

Questions: *What is an order and reply to an order? And how do you write an order and reply to an order?*

① Orders and Replies

    An order is a request to supply a specified quantity of goods. Very often, it is only after the exchange of a number of letters, faxes or e-mails that the two parties come entirely to terms and the buyer finally places or fills a formal order. Sometimes a buyer may take the initiative by placing a firm order with the seller, which is a firm bid to buy something and contains all necessary terms and conditions. Usually a formal order should

contain:
- name of commodity, article number, specification, etc.;
- quantity;
- delivery date and port of destination;
- unit price, total amount, and price terms;
- payment terms, etc.

When a seller receives the relative order and accepts its terms and conditions, he may begin to execute the order to the buyer's satisfaction. However, there are times when the seller does not accept the buyer's order for some of the following reasons:
* The seller is not satisfied with the buyer's terms and conditions;
* The buyer's credit is suspect;
* The goods are not available.

Letters declining an order for the above reasons should be written with utmost care and an eye to goodwill and future business.

② Points to Remember

The essential qualities of an order are accuracy and clarity. In an order letter, you are required to supply the following information as exactly as possible: description of the goods, destination of the order shipped, payment and any special circumstances.

Many companies now use printed order forms/sheets which ensure that all the necessary information is given. You should accompany the order form with a letter. This accompanying letter is called a cover letter.

When you write an order letter, you ought to follow the following steps:
- Open with reference to some previous contacts such as catalogs, phone calls, exhibitions or trade fairs. This helps the reader find out the intention of the letter.
- Describe the order.
- Mention payment and delivery.
- Express courtesy.

When a company receives an order letter or order form, it often responds with a confirmation letter. A confirmation letter must be clear and specific about what is being confirmed or what is being changed.

When you write a positive confirmation letter, you usually include the following parts:
- Thanks for the order
- Favorable comment on the items required
- Assurance of the best attention
- Other items which may be of interest to the customer
- Hope for further order

When you are unable to accept the order, you should reply in time either to decline the order or to make a counter-offer.

- Thanks for the order
- Proper reasons to decline the order with regret
- Recommendation of other items as a replacement or presentation of counter-offer
- Hope for serving the customer in the future

B. Experience by reading and answering questions.

a. Read the following order letter and answer questions.
- *How do you like the order? Is it an offer to the seller from the buyer?*
- *How do you like the delivery date asked for by the buyer?*

Gentlemen,

Thank you for your quotation of July 25 together with patterns of Printed Shirting. We find both quality and price satisfactory and are pleased to give you an order for the following items on the understanding that they will be supplied from stock at the prices named:

Quantity	Pattern No.	Prices
50,000 yards	181	HK $11 per yd.
40,000 yards	183	HK $14 per yd.
50,000 yards	185	HK $17 per yd.

(All the prices are FOB Hong Kong.)

We expect to find a good market for the above and hope to place further and large orders with you in the near future.

Our usual terms of payment are by D/P 60 days and we hope they will be satisfactory to you. Meanwhile, should you wish to make enquiries concerning our financial standing, you may refer to the following bank:

The A. B. C. Bank
15XYZ Street, Hong Kong.

All these items are urgently required by our customers. We, therefore, hope you will make delivery at an early date.

Yours sincerely,
[Signature]

---

b. Read the following letter and answer questions.
- *Does the seller agree to sell the goods? What about the delivery date?*
- *Is the seller an astute businessman? How?*

Dear Sirs,

Thank you for your order for Printed Shirting and you are welcome as one of our customers.

We confirm our acceptance of the order at the prices mentioned in your letter and subject to your agreement that delivery of the goods is to be made in May. We have confidence that the goods will turn out to your complete satisfaction when the goods reach you. They represent exceptional value at their prices. We are confident that you will have a good turnover, and that you will be able to place repeat orders with us very soon.

Besides the Printed Shirting we supply a wide range of other goods of which you may not be aware. Enclosed is a copy of our current catalogue and price list. Should you be interested in any of them, we shall be glad to send you patterns.

We hope that our handling of your first order will pave the way for further development of business between us and mark the beginning of a satisfactory working relationship.

Yours sincerely,

[Signature]

6.1.2 Practice

☞ **A. Read the following conversation and then complete the order sheet on its basis.**

Leslie: How are you this afternoon?

Paul: Just fine. I looked over the catalogue you gave me this morning, and I'd like to discuss your computer speakers.

Leslie: Very good. Here is our price list.

Paul: Let me see ... I see that your listed price for the K-2-1 model is ten US dollars. Do you offer quantity discounts?

Leslie: We sure do. We give a five percent discount for orders of a hundred or more.

Paul: What kind of discount could you give me if I were to place an order for six hundred units?

Leslie: On an order of six hundred units, we can give you a discount of ten percent.

Paul: What about lead time?

Leslie: We could ship your order within ten days of receiving your payment.

Paul: So, you require payment in advance of shipment?

Leslie: Yes. You could wire transfer the payment into our bank account or open a letter of credit in our favour.

Paul: I'd like to go ahead and place an order for six hundred units.

Leslie: Great! I'll just fill out the purchase order and have you sign it.

Order Sheet

No.:
Date:

Dear Sirs,

We have the pleasure to place with you our order for the undermentioned goods on the terms and conditions stated as follows:

➢ Name of Commodity and Specifications:
➢ Quantity:
➢ Price and Total Amount:
  a. Price:
  b. Total Amount:

> Packing: To be packed in wooden cases, suitable for export
> Shipment: To be effected
> Destination: New York
> Insurance: To be effected by the Seller, covering marine All Risks and War Risk for 110% CIF value
> Payment:
> Shipping Mark: ABC: New York (1-600)

We are going to instruct our bank to open a letter of credit for the amount of this order. You will soon hear from your bank.

                                  Yours faithfully,
                                  [Signature]

Accepted by:
  (Seller)   (Buyer)
  (Signature)   (Signature)

B. Read the order letter in the following and make your comment. Then complete the reply, refusing to execute the order but offering to supply substitutes.

Dear Sirs,

Order of Fashion Blouse A437

Thank you very much for your offer of May 12 and the sample blouses. We find both quality and prices satisfactory and are pleased to place an order with you for the following:

Commodity: Fashion Blouse A437, Size 38

Quantity: 100 dozens

Packing: Each blouse to be packed in a polybag, per dozen in a cardboard carton, with 10 cartons in a wooden case

Other terms according to your offer.

We expect to find a good market for the above and hope to place further and large orders with you in the near future.

                                  Yours sincerely,
                                  [Signature]

Reply to the above order letter

Dear Sirs,

Thank you for your order of May 20.

We should like to fill your order for the Fashion Blouse A437, Size 38, _____ ① _____ (但是,我们收到的订单比我们预料的多,以至于我们大量的存货已经售罄).

The manufacturer is no longer able to supply this blouse, _____ ② _____ (但是,幸运的是我们现货有一种质量同样高、式样同样精致的女式衬衣,而价格稍低).

You will find this blouse listed and illustrated in our catalogue, on Page 15, A438. We can send you the blouse promptly _____③_____ (如果我们几天内收到你们的订单). This model is very popular. It is now selling as fast as the model you ordered.

Remember, you are fully protected by our guarantee: "Money cheerfully and promptly refunded if you are not satisfied". We are certain, however, that _____④_____ (你们将爱不释手).

Please write the catalogue number of the blouse and the size you desire on enclosed special order blank, and mail it to us in the enclosed stamped envelope.

The blouse will reach you promptly.

Yours sincerely,
[Signature]

6.1.3 Case study & practice

☞ **A. Read the following and rearrange them in the right order.**

Gentlemen,

① Shipment: Within 45 days after receipt of the relevant L/C

② Packing: Each set is to be wrapped in a poly bag and packed in a standard carton lined with foam

③ Price: US $700.00 per set CIF Guangzhou, China

④ Quantity: 300 sets

⑤ Name of commodity: IBM Personal Computers, CPU80686

⑥ There is a great demand for your products here, so prompt delivery will be most appreciated.

⑦ We are fully confident that you will pay special attention to the packing of the goods in case they should be damaged in transit. After receiving your sales confirmation, we will establish the L/C. Meanwhile, please note that shipment must be effected within the validity of our L/C. If the shipment comes up to our expectation, substantial orders will follow.

⑧ Referring to the faxes exchanged between us recently, we confirm the following order placed with you:

Faithfully yours,
[Signature]

☞ **B. Write a reply to the above letter according to the given directions.**

- Express your thanks for the order you've received.
- Say you accept the order and you've enclosed the S/C in the reply.
- Promise that you will take special care of the packing.
- Promise that you will arrange the production right away after receiving the L/C and make delivery within its validity.

6.2 Communicating & Writing Skills

☞ **A. Read and learn how to place or confirm orders.**

◇ **A letter of placing an order**

Dear Sirs,

We thank you for your quotation of October 3 and the sample garments you sent us. We find both quality and prices satisfactory and would like to place an order with you for the following:

    1,000   MJ Blouses (five colors and five sizes)
    2,000   CP Jackets (also five colors and five sizes)

The terms agreed upon with Mr Wang during my telephone conversation this morning are as follows:

  a. Prices as stated in your quotation of October 3 to include delivery to final destination.
  b. Payment to be made in Pound Sterling to your London representative within one month of the arrival of the goods at Liverpool.
  c. Insurance to be arranged by you with a Lloyd's broker through your London representative.

We should appreciate prompt shipment and hope to establish a regular connection for the future if this first consignment proves to conform to the samples supplied.

                                                                Yours faithfully,
                                                                [Signature]

◇ **A letter of confirming an order**

Dear Sirs,

Against the subject order from you we are pleased to enclose our Sales Confirmation No. EH-718 for your signature. You are asked to return us a copy as soon as possible.

While thanking you for the confidence you have placed in us, we wish to add that according to our usual practice we use the form of Sales Confirmation for confirming the conclusion of business rather than sign the Order Form of our clients. Our Sales Confirmations are reliable instruments which accurately and comprehensively show the spirit and essence of our agreement. To abide by the stipulations and carry them out to the full will mean the complete realization of the duties and rights of both parties to the mutual benefit. We hope that this explanation will meet with your approval.

If there should be any question about the wording or content of the terms and stipulations, please tell us so that we may make a check or change, if necessary.

                                                                 Yours sincerely,
                                                                [Signature]

Study the following examples.

- Expressions of placing an order

a) Thank you for your offer of February 14. Your prices and quality turned out to be satisfactory and we are sending you an order for the following.

b) We are pleased to enclose an indent/trial order/purchase order/revised order/substitute order for 20,000 pieces of plastic toy mobile phones.

c) We are pleased to place an order with you for the following household electric appliances.

d) With reference to our order for leather shoes we have pleasure in sending you our Purchase Confirmation No. 357 in triplicate, one copy of which please sign and return to us.

- Expressions of confirming an order

a) We are writing to confirm our telephone call this morning ordering the following items.

b) We confirm having purchased from you 20,000 dozens of pencils, for which a confirmation of order is enclosed for your reference.

c) Enclosed is our Confirmation of Order in duplicate, of which please return us one copy duly signed.

B. Read the following e-mail of increasing order and observe how to make requests related to one's order.

To: Sam Yen / SNC Co.
From: Claude / Laub Technology
Date: June 28, 2021
Re: PO 17003
(1) Currently quantity on the order is 2,000 pcs, our customer needs to increase to 4,000 pcs.
(2) Your shipping date of 7/26 is not good enough, the customer needs all 4,000 pcs much sooner. What can you do to improve the shipping date? We need all 4,000 pcs via air.
Please review and advise your very best shipping date by return. Thanks.

Write something in the following situations.

a) Ask the seller to make sure that the goods meet your requirements.

b) Tell the seller to supply the substitutes if he cannot supply goods per the enclosed specifications.

c) Urge the seller to arrange for the ordered goods to reach you by the end of this month.

d) Ask the seller to guarantee that the goods are absolutely waterproof.

e) Stress your condition that the goods are dispatched in time to reach you by September 15. Add that you reserve the right to cancel it and to refuse delivery after this date.

C. Read the following letters and observe how to accept and decline an order.

◇ A letter of accepting an order

Dear Ms Trask,

<u>Re: Your Order No. 16</u>

We have accepted your Order No. 16 for handkerchiefs, leather shoes and socks and are sending you herewith our Sales Confirmation No. Garm-263 in duplicate. Would you please sign and return one copy to us for file?

It is understood that a letter of credit in our favor covering the above-mentioned goods will be established at once. Please note that the stipulations in the relevant credit should strictly conform to the terms stated in our Sales Confirmation so as to avoid subsequent amendments. You may rest assured that we shall effect shipment with the least possible delay upon receipt of the credit.

We appreciate your cooperation and look forward to receiving your further orders.

Faithfully yours,

Mary Lin

◇ An e-mail of declining an order

To: Mr Brad Lois / OBA Trading Co.
From: Peter Lee / JC Corp.
Re: Your P. O. #B1852
Date: March 22, 2021

We received your above order today, in which you confirmed the quantity of two containers only.

As offered in our last correspondence, we would give you 1.5% discount only based on the order for total 3 containers. So, please reconfirm if you want to increase the quantity to 3 containers to get the 1.5% discount, or only order 2 containers without any discount.

We are waiting for your reply soon.

Sincerely yours,

Peter Lee

Rearrange the mixed-up words or expressions into order.

a) give our best and prompt attention to / we shall / this order / the execution of

b) that / you / we assure / the order / handled / will be / with great care

c) every effort / we shall / to ship the goods / on time / feel sure that / will be / the shipment / satisfactory / to you / make / and

d) your order / we have accepted / for 30,000 yards of Article No. 57 / according to the terms contracted / color assortment / please send us / immediately / and / the covering Letter of Credit / open

e) as specified in your order of May 24 / accept / we are not / unfortunately / in a position to / the conditions of payment and delivery / we would be happy / under the conditions customary in our trade / however / to accept your order

f) we cannot accept / unfortunately / your order / on the specified conditions / of August 8

g) to manufacture / we are unable / the article you ordered / we are returning / enclosed / your order

h) of June 19 / we cannot accept / due to shortage of trained help / your order

i) we cannot accept / has been committed to other orders / because our supply of raw materials / for months in advance / your order / at present

j) we are unable to / due to difficulties with our suppliers / at this time / accept your order

☞ **D. Read the following letter and observe how to give reasons for refusing or declining orders.**

Dear Mr Kirkpatrick,

We acknowledge receipt of your order No.1315 for 200 air-conditioners. Much to our regret, we cannot at present entertain your order owing to shortage of stocks.

In the meantime because of the fluctuation of the price of raw materials, we are now adjusting our price list. We will, however, send you quotations as soon as your ordered goods are available and the price list is settled. We sincerely regret any inconvenience you may have experienced. You can rely on our best attention at all times.

Yours faithfully,

Sam Song

Write something in the following situations.

1) Say that your factory is fully engaged and cannot take on fresh orders.

2) Say that you have so many orders on your hands that you cannot entertain fresh business.

3) Apologize that for the moment you cannot accept orders for delivery this year.

4) Say that you have to reject the order of July 7 for you have difficulties in obtaining the materials needed for the order.

5) Tell the buyer that you cannot accept the order owing to heavy sales.

6.3 Writers' Workshop: Textual Development of Letters (1)

Approaches for Textual Development

As ESP, Business English is used in various kinds of formal and informal practical writings, which are mostly expository and partly argumentative, such as business letters, memos, reports and contracts.

When you do such practical writings for expository textual building, you mainly apply such development approaches as persuasion, cause-effect, comparison-contrast, process analysis and listing. As a result, you may develop your letters either in inductive or in deductive pattern of organization.

Inductive and Deductive Patterns

You can't let your readers get confused when you move from one point to the next or when you change the direction of your ideas. In other words, your message should be so well organized that there is unity and coherence in it. A good method to achieve unity and coherence is to make a mental or written outline before writing. There are two basic patterns to follow in organizing your ideas: inductive and deductive patterns.

Inductive organization is also known as the indirect pattern that means beginning with the specific facts that are obvious and moving to a general conclusion. The following example shows how this pattern functions.

    Facts: a. Today, the outdoor temperature is 33.
           b. The temperature in my office today is 30.
           c. No air is circulating in my office.
    Conclusion: The air-conditioner in my office isn't functioning today.

Deductive organization is also called the direct pattern. This pattern begins with a conclusion, and works backward to try to find the facts on which the conclusions are based. For the same situation, the deductive pattern would be:

    Conclusion: The air-conditioner in my office isn't functioning today because …
    Facts: a. No air is circulating in my office.
           b. The temperature in my office today is 30.
           c. Today, the outdoor temperature is 33.

Here, we won't analyze which pattern we will use. We simply know that for certain types of information, one pattern is better than the other. For example, favorable messages follow the deductive pattern or the direct approach, while unfavorable messages use the inductive pattern or the indirect approach.

Be aware of the two basic patterns and choose a suitable one in organizing your ideas to assure that your reader will understand how each idea relates to the others in your message.

6.3.1 Group work

Work in groups of 3 or 4 to discuss the proper arrangement of the different parts of a message.

    a) Necessary explanation
    b) Series of additional questions
    c) Goodwill close
    d) Direct request

6.3.2 Reading and comparing the different patterns of textual organisation and their effects.

Letter 1

Dear Susan,

The idea of starting an online toy store did not seem workable just after the burst of the "dot com" bubble. However, several on line stores are still doing well, largely due to thoughtful customer-focused services, user-friendly transactions and reliable technical support. Unlike several "comet" IT companies that entered too hastily into multiple businesses, surviving companies have expanded their products and services with caution and realism. The benefits, as we all know, have been enormous.

I therefore believe that if we apply the same thoughtful principles, this would be the right moment to open an online toy store. A particularly interesting trend is that customers like to share their toy-selecting experiences with each other. We could thus provide a unique online service that local shops, no matter how diversified in other ways, would have difficulty competing with.

In short, I would be very happy to consider opening an online toy store with you and look forward to discussing this possibility in more details.

Best regards,
Pauline

Letter 2

Dear Susan,

Thank you for your e-mail of February 5.

Opening an online toy store together sounds like an excellent idea, as you have the IT expertise and I have the marketing experience.

Moreover, despite the burst of the "dot com" bubble, several online stores are actually doing quite well. I can think of three main reasons for their success: thoughtful customer-focused services, user-friendly trading and reliable technical support. IT companies that failed in the past either did not pay sufficient attention to these key elements or entered too hastily into multiple lines of business. A natural result was confused market positioning and diminishing capital.

We could open an online toy store that encourages customers to exchange their toy-selecting experiences, which in turn would enable us to improve our services through real-time feedback. Opening channel of communication between customers would be a wonderful IT forward that local shops, no matter how diversified in other ways, cannot provide.

If you share my ideas, I would like to discuss this opportunity in more details and look forward to your comments.

Best regards,
Pauline

6.3.3 Comment and improvement
Comment on the following letter and improve it.

Dear Jeremy,

    I won't bore you with the details but the bottom line is someone in inventory control (who was terminated as a result) wasn't doing his job and we've run out of stock on several important items unexpectedly. Needless to say we're in "crisis mode" and we depend on you to fill the attached order at once. Please call if there's a problem with this.

                                                   Sincerely yours,

                                                   Dustin Bodack

Unit 7 Payment & Replies

Learning Objectives

- ✓ learning about different means of international payment
- ✓ learning how to negotiate about international payment
- ✓ learning how to perform relative functions of language and communication
- ✓ learning how to write in direct and indirect ways

Identify Problems in the Following Writing & Comment

Dear Mr Smith,

    I saw your request for a proposal in *Tech News*. You didn't say how much you were paying for the training. I need to know whether it's worthwhile to send in a proposal. You can e-mail me at Al-Harrison@ earthlink. net.

    Thanks.

Sincerely,
Allen Harrison

7.1 Experience & Practice

7.1.1 Learning about different means of international payment

A. Brief introduction

Questions: *What are the different means of international payment? What is the safest method of payment? What method of payment is becoming more and more popular in China's foreign trade?*

① Main Means of Payment

Payment is very important in international trade. The final result of business activities is to get the payment for the goods sold or services rendered. Otherwise, all would be of no meaning. So proper means of payment should be chosen to ensure the payment. Generally speaking, payment in international commerce can be made by using remittance, collection and letter of credit.

- Remittance

Remittance means that the debtor (the importer) remits the amount of money to the creditor (the exporter) through banks. There are three kinds of remittance. Mail Transfer (M/T), Telegraphic Transfer (T/T) and Remittance by Banker's Demand Draft (D/D).

- Collection

Collection means that the exporter draws a draft according to the invoice and then instructs the bank to collect the amount of money in question from the importer. There are two kinds of international collection: Clean Collection and Documentary Collection. In most cases, the latter is more often employed for payment. Documentary Collection can be divided into two groups: Documents against Acceptance (D/A) and Documents against Payment (D/P).

- Letter of credit

The letter of credit is the most widely-used and secure method of payment in international trade. It's a kind of bank credit instead of commercial credit like remittance or collection.

A letter of credit is a written document issued by the buyer's bank that promises that the bank will pay the seller the agreed amount of money, providing that all the requirements of the letter of credit are met. These requirements generally include delivery dates; product specifications; the receipt by the bank of certain documents within a specified period of time, etc. If the letter of credit should be against the contract and the documents, the exporter will ask the importer to make amendments to the L/C.

There are many kinds of letters of credit: Documentary L/C, Clean L/C; Irrevocable L/C, Revocable L/C; Confirmed L/C, Unconfirmed L/C; Sight L/C, Usance L/C; Transferable L/C, Non-transferable L/C; Revolving L/C, Anticipatory L/C, Negotiation L/C, Acceptance L/C, etc.

② Other Means of Payment

In addition to the above 3 most common methods, other means are employed in international payment.

- Cash in advance

It is, of course, the most desirable means of receiving payment. At the same time, it is a very unattractive payment term to the buyer. Unless an order is very small, the foreign buyer will be tying up substantial capital over a considerable length of time before the merchandise is received. The buyer is also dependent on the seller's honesty, solvency, and promptness in the transaction. Furthermore, the buyer may resent the implication that he may not be credit-worthy.

Because of the fierce competition of international trade, the seller's ability and willingness to offer buyers credit can often determine whether they win the sale.

- Open-account sales

Exporters commonly use open-account sales when transacting business with a well-established, reputable, and familiar buyer. The principal advantage of this method is its ease and convenience. However, because there is no negotiable instrument to document the sale, difficult collection problems result if the buyer refuses to pay the bill.

With open-account sales, the sellers bear the burden of financing the shipment. The standard practice in many countries is to wait until the merchandise is sold, delaying payment even longer. Consequently, among the various forms of payment, open-account sales require the greatest amount of working capital. Additionally, the sellers bear the exchange risk if the sales are quoted in a foreign currency. Despite all these disadvantages, competitive pressures may force the sellers to use this method.

③ Points to Remember

When you write letters of payment, remember to follow the following pattern:

- In the opening paragraph, state directly and clearly which letter you are referring to.
- In the middle part, mention the method of payment your company usually adopts, things about payment documents or accounts due, mistakes or misunderstanding in the accounts, and suggestions to solve the problem, etc.
- In the closing part, express your hope that the method of payment will be acceptable to your business partner.

B. Experience by reading and answering questions.

a. Read the following letter and answer the questions.

- *How about the payment by L/C? Is it a sight one or a usance one?*
- *Is a usance L/C good to the buyer or the seller? Why?*

⊕ **Suggestion for payment by usance L/C**

Dear Sirs,

We would like to place an order for 600 Flyingfish 161 electric typewriters at your price of US $300.00 each, CIF Lagos, for shipment during July/August.

We would like to pay for this order by a 30-day L/C. This is a big order involving US $150,000 and payment by L/C would tie up funds for three or four months, which would cause problems for us as we have only moderate cash reserves.

If you agree, please send us your contract. On receipt, we will establish the relevant L/C immediately.

We hope that you can make prompt delivery of our order.

Yours sincerely,

[Signature]

b. Read the following letter and answer the questions.

- *Does the writer accept the buyer's suggestion to pay by a usance L/C?*
- *What does the seller say as a reminder?*

⊕ **Reply to suggestion for payment by usance L/C**

Dear Sirs,

Thank you for your order for 600 Flyingfish 161 typewriters by your letter of May 20.

We have considered your proposal to pay by a 30-day letter of credit. We do not usually accept time credit. However, in view of our long and mutually beneficial relationship, we are willing to make an exception this time. But it cannot be seen as setting a precedent for future transactions.

I enclose our Sales Contract No. 63 covering the order. I would be grateful if you would follow the usual procedure.

Yours sincerely,
[Signature]

c. Read the following letter and answer the questions.
- *What does the writer write the letter for?*
- *What kind of businessman is the writer? What does he ask for?*

⊕ **A letter advising to establish letter of credit**

Dear Sirs,

We are pleased to tell you that we have secured Three Orders, the particulars of which are to be given in the separate air letter we are posting today.

Please send us as soon as possible a Sales Note per the prices indicated by us in the Indents, and a further document showing the extra amount and commission due to us on each Indent. As soon as we receive these, we shall establish a letter of credit in your favor.

Looking forward to your reply.

Yours faithfully,
[Signature]

d. Read the following letter and answer the questions.
- *What does the writer write the letter for?*
- *Is the letter a courteous one?*

⊕ **A letter urging the establishement of L/C**

Dear Mr Liemens,

We wish to inform you that the goods under S/C Nos 2354 and 2355 have been ready for quite some time. According to the stipulations in the foregoing sales confirmations, shipment is to be made during June/July.

We sent you a fax two weeks ago asking you to expedite the relevant L/C. The fax reads:

The goods under S/C Nos 2354 and 2355 have been ready. Please open L/C immediately.

But to our disappointment, we have not received any reply up to now.

The shipment date is approaching. We must point out that unless your L/C reaches us by the end of this month, we shall not be able to effect shipment within the stipulated time limit.

You might recall the following points concerning the establishment of L/C as stated in our previous correspondence:

- Ls/C with details should reach us one month preceding the month of shipment;
- Ls/C must be made as concise as possible. When establishing the L/C, please make sure the L/C stipulations are in exact accordance with the terms set forth in our sales confirmation.

We hope this letter will receive your prompt attention and look forward to receiving your favorable news in the shortest possible time.

Faithfully yours,
He Xueqing

e. Read the following letter and answer the questions.
- *What is the letter written for?*
- *What does the buyer ask for at the end of the letter?*

⊕ **Reply to a letter urging the establishment of L/C**

Dear Mr Ho,

Thank you for your letter of May 18 and the L/C in question has already been opened and sent.

For your information, we are enclosing a photo static copy of Document Credit No. 6574 – FE dated May 25, covering the following two specific sales confirmations:

S/C No. 2354 US $50,430 Toys
S/C No. 2355 US $40,500 Stationery

Please verify the matter with your bank. We are pleased to learn that the goods we ordered are ready for dispatch and hope you will inform us at your earliest convenience of the name of the carrying vessel and its sailing date.

Sincerely yours,
E. Liemens

7.1.2 Practice

A. Read the following conversation and then on Mary Lublin's behalf, write a letter on its basis.

Mr Murry: Now that the price has been settled, let's go on to the terms of payment.

Mary Lublin: Sure. As you've seen from specimen contract, we require payment by L/C payable against presentation of shipping documents.

Mr Murry: Could you make an exception in your case and accept D/A?

Mary Lublin: As a rule, we ask for payment by L/C. But in view of our long business relations, we will, as an exceptional case, accept payment for your order by D/P at sight.

Mr Murry: It's very kind of you. We'll place our order with you very soon.

Mary Lublin: Thanks.

B. Read the following letter and make your comment. Then write a reply.

Dear Sirs,

We have examined the specifications and price list for your range of colored candles, and now wish to place an order with you. We enclose our order No. 569 for 2,000 dozen candles.

As we are in urgent need of candles for the coming holiday season, we would be grateful if you would make up the order and ship it as soon as possible.

In the past we have traded with you on a sight credit basis. We would now like to propose a different arrangement. When the goods are ready for shipment and the freight space booked, you will fax us and we will then remit the full amount by telegraphic transfer (T/T).

We are asking for this concession so that we can give our customers a specific delivery date and also save the expenses of opening a letter of credit. As we believe that this arrangement should make little difference to you and help with our sales, we trust that you will agree to our request.

We look forward to receiving confirmation of order and your agreement to the new arrangements for payment.

Yours truly,
John Marlow
Manager

7.1.3 Case study & practice

Write a letter asking for amendment to the covering L/C according to the general idea given below:

◇ **Topic:** Thanks for the L/C No. TK 309 covering the Order No. 9008 of December 16 for 630 metric tons of the contracted goods. Ask for amendment to the L/C.

◇ **Explanation:** It is wrong that the L/C calls for a material of 65%, which should be 63.5%. Besides, the L/C ought to require the goods to be packed in 160 kg drums instead of in 100 kg drums.

◇ **Conclusion:** Please see to it that future credits are correct in every way and amend the covering L/C at once.

7.2 Communicating & Writing Skills

☞ **A. Read the following letters and learn how to negotiate the terms of payment.**

Letter 1

Dear Mr Muller,

We are pleased to receive your enquiry of July 5 and enclose our illustrated catalogue and price list.

We are confident you will be interested in our products and welcome your further enquiry.

As to our terms of payment, we usually adopt confirmed, irrevocable letters of credit in our favor, payable by draft at sight, reaching us one month ahead of shipment, remaining valid for negotiation in China for a further 21 days after prescribed time of shipment and allowing transshipment and partial shipment.

We hope the above payment terms will be acceptable to you and expect to receive your trial order soon.

Sincerely yours,
Alex Wang

Unit 7 Payment & Replies

Letter 2

Dear Sirs,

Re: 2000 dz PUMA shoes

Thank you for your letter of May 9 in which we have concluded a transaction of 2,000 dozens of PUMA brand shoes. But to our regret, you still ask for payment by confirmed irrevocable L/C as a rule.

Payment by L/C is rather inconvenient to a customer like us who places medium-sized orders. It will add to our cost and undoubtedly tie up our liquid funds for three or four months. This may cause delay in execution of the contract. The question becomes gnawing under present circumstances.

In view of our long business relationship and the small amount involved in this transaction, we hope you will extend us an easier payment terms as an exception, i.e. payment by D/A. Your accommodation would be conducive to the future business and facilitates us promoting your products in our market.

We shall highly appreciate your kindness in consideration of the above request and giving us a favorable reply.

Yours faithfully,
Amtrade International Co., Ltd.
John Stewart

Match the parts in the first group with those in the second one.

1) As agreed, the terms of payment are
2) As agreed, payment is to
3) As agreed,
4) As agreed, we only
5) As agreed, we can

a. be made against sight draft under L/C
b. by irrevocable L/C, payable by sight draft
c. require 100% value, confirmed and irrevocable L/C payable at sight
d. not accept cash against documents on arrival of goods at destination
e. our business terms are D/P sight draft

☞ **B. Read the following letters and learn how to urge the establishment of L/C.**

Letter 1

Dear Sirs,

According to our S/C, your L/C should have reached us before the end of last month. We regret to say we haven't received it now. Please expedite the establishment of the relevant L/C upon receipt of this letter so that we can effect shipment in time.

We are awaiting your early reply.

Yours sincerely,
[Signature]

A Coursebook for Business English Writing

Letter 2

Dear Sirs,

Re: S/C No. G556

With reference to the correspondences exchanged between us recently, we have finalized the business on the basis of FOB. Needless to say that as a buyer, you are responsible for applying for an L/C, but much to our disappointment we have not had any news from you though we sent you an e-mail two weeks ago pressing you for opening.

We have got the goods ready for shipment for quite some time. As contracted, the relative L/C covering the above should have reached us before the end of last week. As the date of delivery is only one month and half away, we recommend that you open the L/C without delay. Extra charges and any losses caused by delay of arrival of L/C will be for your account.

Please open your L/C immediately and let us have your reply by return. Your prompt attention to this matter will be appreciated.

Yours truly,
[Signature]

Translate the Chinese into English in the following sentences.

1) We should request you to _____（速开信用证）so that we may effect shipment by the direct steamer scheduled to arrive here about October 10.

2) As the goods ordered are ready for shipment, please expedite your L/C. _____ _____（信用证一到,我们就装船发货）.

3) As the goods against your Order No. 4564 have been ready for shipment for quite some time, it is imperative that you _____（迅速采取行动）to have the covering L/C established as soon as possible.

4) With reference to your Indent NO. 5218, we have not yet received the relative L/C. As this order has been outstanding for considerable time, we would ask you to _____（马上关注此事）.

☞ **C. Read the following letters and learn how to ask for amendment to L/C.**

Letter 1

Dear Sirs,

Would you amend the L/C No. 124/12 to allow transshipment for our mutual benefit?

Thank you for your L/C No. 124/12 issued by the National Bank, Greensboro, for the amount of $ 13,567 covering 1,000 dozen children toy cars.

The said L/C reached us yesterday. On perusal, we find that transshipment and partial shipment are not allowed. But as there are few direct steamers to your port, it is almost impossible for us to effect shipment under such circumstances.

Our usual practice is to ship via Hong Kong. So it is imperative to amend the L/C to read TRASNSHIMENT AND PARTIAL SHIMEENT ALLOWED.

Please send the amendment by cable without any delay as the goods have been packed for shipment. Your understanding and cooperation are highly appreciated.

Yours faithfully,
James Zhao

Letter 2

Dear Sirs,

We refer to the 1,500 dozen shirts under our S/C No. TS121 and wish to point out that the time of shipment is approaching, but we found surprisingly there are several points in the L/C not in conformity with what stipulated in the contract as follows:

1) The amount of your L/C is insufficient. The total amount is USD $ 2,100 instead of USD $ 2,000.
2) Please delete the clause "by direct steamer" and insert the wording "transshipment and partial shipment are allowed".
3) The validity of L/C is 20 days after shipment.

We shall highly appreciate it if you pay prompt attentions to this matter and give us response at the earliest convenience.

Yours faithfully,
[Signature]

Study the following examples.

1) As there is no direct steamer available this month, we should like to request you <u>to extend the validity of your L/C No. 3792 to the end of May</u>.
2) Your L/C No. 5802 has just been received. Since the date of shipment mentioned in the said L/C is July 16 leaving only 3 days for us to arrange shipment, it is impossible to meet. We request you <u>to extend it to July 28</u>. Please note that this is a matter over which we can exercise no control.
3) Please ask the bank <u>to amend Credit No. 6219 to read: "Joint Bills of Lading with Credit No. 6219 acceptable"</u>.
4) We have received your L/C No. 7249 but find that it contains the following discrepancies: We request you <u>to instruct your bankers to make the necessary amendment to the L/C</u>.
5) <u>Please delete "fresh water damage" from the L/C</u>.

D. Read and compare the following two letters to ask for settlement of overdue account.

Letter 1

Dear Mr Cheng,

ACCOUNT NO. 0576

As we have always received your payment punctually, we wonder if there is any special reason to have caused your account to be one month overdue. We guess you may not have received the statement of account sent by our account department on 30 June. We therefore enclose a copy which shows that there is a balance of HK $7,490.

Kindly recheck with your account department. Your prompt action is highly appreciated.

Yours sincerely,
Helen Tang

Letter 2

Dear Mr Lam,

We have still received no reply from you concerning our letter of 4 and 20 January requesting the settlement of the overdue amount HK $ 250,000.

We therefore regret that we have no choice but to request you to settle the payment immediately. Otherwise we will take further steps in order to obtain the payment.

Yours sincerely,
Norman Woo

Study examples of warning to overdue account

1) We hope that you will take your commercial reputation into account in all seriousness and open the L/C at once. <u>Otherwise, you will be responsible for all the losses arising therefrom.</u>

2) If you do not establish the L/C in time, <u>you will be responsible for any loss resulting from the delay.</u>

3) Although our business relations in the past few years have always been pleasant, <u>we cannot allow the amount remain unpaid indefinitely. We are reluctantly compelled to turn the matter over to a collection agent if you can't settle it by the end of this week.</u>

☞ **E. Read the following letters to ask for extension or grant amendment to L/C and learn how to make apologies.**

Letter 1

Dear Sirs,

　　We acknowledge with thanks receipt of your L/C No.1123, covering your order for 30 long tons of Bridge brand welding electrodes.

　　We are sorry that, on account of the delay on part of our suppliers at the point of origin, we won't be able to have the goods prepared by the end of March. We thus sent you a fax yesterday, asking for the extension of the shipment date and validity of the credit.

　　It is expected that the consignment will be ready for shipment in the early part of May and we are arranging to ship it on S.S "Fanyang" sailing from Dalian on or about May 10.

　　Thank you for your understanding and cooperation in this matter. We sincerely hope that you would immediately extend your L/C as requested thus enabling us to effect shipment of the goods in question.

　　　　　　　　　　　　　　　　　　　　　　　　　　　　Yours truly,
　　　　　　　　　　　　　　　　　　　　　　　　　　　　[Signature]

Letter 2

Dear Sirs,

　　　　　　　　　　　　　　Re: Amendment to L/C No. 5301

　　Thank you for your letter of June 3, and have to apologize to you for the mistake we've made in the above-mentioned L/C, which is completely due to carelessness.

　　We have already instructed our bank to amend the relevant L/C by fax without the least delay and we are sure the fax amendment will reach you in one or two days. As we need the goods badly, please arrange prompt shipment.

　　　　　　　　　　　　　　　　　　　　　　　　　　　　Yours faithfully,
　　　　　　　　　　　　　　　　　　　　　　　　　　　　[Signature]

　　Translate the following sentences into Chinese, paying special attention to the underlined parts.

1) Upon checking the cause of this delay, we have found that our accounting department made an oversight in making remittance to you. <u>We are sorry for the trouble caused to you by the delay.</u>

2) <u>We apologize for the lateness of this check,</u> which was caused by our oversight. I hope the delay has not brought you any inconvenience.

7.3 Writers' Workshop: Textual Development of Letters (2)

Direct and Indirect Approach

The direct approach means arranging ideas in a direct order, usually beginning with the most important point and working downward. This approach is good for all good news and neutral messages. The direct approach gives the reader the sense of immediacy. By taking your reader directly to the issue in question, you save his time. So in the direct approach, the message is arranged as follows:
- Begin with the main point
- Present the necessary explanation(s)
- Cover the remaining part of the objective
- End with adapted goodwill

The indirect approach is often preferred in writing bad-news messages. As nobody would like to receive a "no" message, a skillful manager will try his best to reduce the negative effects tactfully by arranging the message in an indirect way as follows:
- Begin with a buffer
- Explain why the refusal has to be made
- State the refusal
- Close positively

As can be seen from the above, the direct approach is just the method used to write in the deductive pattern; and the indirect approach the method used to write in the inductive pattern.

7.3.1 Group work

Work in groups of 3 or 4 to arrange the following parts of a routine enquiry message in the correct order.

a) Extra related ideas
b) Cordial, friendly ending
c) Necessary negative information
d) Series of requested answers
e) Single answer or statement of compliance with the request

7.3.2 Reading the beginnings of letters and discussing the function of the buffer with which each of the following letters begin

1) You have every right to expect the best service when you placed your orders so often.

2) Your organization is doing a commendable job educating needy children. You deserve the help of those who are in a position to give it.

3) Your invitation of January 15 to address the National Association of Small Business Owners is a most distinct honor to me personally.

4) We appreciate your concern about the quality of our products.

7.3.3 Comment and improvement

Comment on the following letter and improve it.

Dear Sirs,

We thank you for your Order No. 215 dated March 10, for 6 sets of electric motor cars Model EF-617. We would like to accept your order very much, but we cannot see our way clear to do this. You will understand that the alteration from the standard specifications to your requirements needs a substantial adjustment to our production methods based on the belt conveyor system.

This entails a considerable increase in labor cost and materials. We trust that you will understand that it is not lack of cooperation and goodwill that makes it impossible to meet your wishes. We hope you will find it possible to replace your order by our excellent substitute Model EJ-627.

Yours faithfully,

[Signature]

Unit 8 Shipment & Replies

Learning Objectives

- ✓ learning about international shipment, partial shipment, transshipment, and the bill of lading
- ✓ learning how to negotiate about international shipment
- ✓ learning how to perform relative functions of language and communication
- ✓ learning about the 3 functions and 6 C's of BE writing

Identify Problems in the Following Writing & Comment

Thank you for the time and effort you put into the proposal you placed on my desk last Tuesday. I have very thoughtfully considered your proposal to split the current and continuing Formatting and Design team into two concurrently functioning teams. I have thought about the positive and negative consequences of making such a split, and I have come to the conclusion that the team should continue to work together, as unit.

Allow me to explain my reasons. First, though formatting and design are certainly very distinct, different and unique processes, in my opinion they function well together as a team. The design of a publication can not progress or move forward without understanding the limits, boundaries and barriers of its formatting. Formatting provides the organization, hierarchy and flow which the design team needs to understand in order to create the clear, non-distracting, but beautiful layouts for which we are famous.

8.1 Experience & Practice

8.1.1 Learning about international shipment

☞ **A. Brief introduction**

Questions: What is the international shipment like? And what is partial shipment, transshipment, and the bill of lading?

① International Shipment

Shipment plays a very important role in foreign trade because, without it, transactions can't be concluded, goods sold by the seller cannot be delivered to the buyer abroad and circulation of commodities between countries or regions cannot be realised. Although most of the shipment is often effected by shipping or forwarding agents, businessmen will find it helpful to have a fairly good knowledge of the details regarding the procedures of shipment, the relative shipping documents in order to fulfill an export transaction and effect shipment in a safe, speedy, accurate and economical way.

There are several means of transport (by sea, by air, by rail and by container ships, etc.) in foreign trade. As about 98% of world trade is covered by sea transport, exporters and importers are more concerned with transport by sea than in other ways. Transport by air is, however, increasing in scope and is the best method for certain types of export and import and under emergency circumstances, though its limitations are obvious. The modern way of transportation is that the cargo is transported by container ships.

After making shipment, the seller should promptly advise the buyer of its effectuation, no matter whether the transaction is concluded on FOB, CFR or CIF basis. For FOB and CFR transactions, the buyer will have to effect insurance on the shipment upon receipt of shipping advice from the seller. It has been a customary practice that in the case of FOB transactions, the seller, before shipping, should ask the buyer to name the vessel on which the goods are to be shipped unless otherwise specified in the contract or L/C.

② The Bill of Lading, Partial Shipment and Transshipment

Usually, the consignor, carrier and consignee are the three parties involved in shipment of goods. The bill of lading, an essential document in making shipment, serves as a receipt of goods signed by the shipping company (carrier) and given to the consignor and is also a contract of carriage between the carrier and the consignor. With the expansion of international trade, the container service has now become quite popular.

Provided that the nature of the goods permits and that appropriate stipulations have been laid down in the contract or L/C, the seller may choose to make several partial shipments. In case where direct sailing from one port to the other is unavailable, transshipment is necessary. As such, the stipulation "transshipment is allowed" should be laid down in the L/C and in the contract.

③ Points to Remember

When you write shipment letters, you ought to follow the steps below:

✓ Open with reference to former contact, or open with a statement, usually about an order, by indicating the number or date of the order.

✓ Give information about the shipment.

✓ Expect either an answer or further communication.

B. Experience by reading and answering questions.

a. Read the following letter and answer the questions.

- *What is the letter written about?*
- *What is the writer anxious to do? Why does the buyer write the letter?*

> Dear Sirs,
>
> We refer to Contract No. 8524 covering 700 dozen track suits. Up to now, we have had no news from you about shipment of the goods.
>
> As we mentioned in our last letter, we need the goods urgently and we may be compelled to seek an alternative source of supply.
>
> Under the circumstances, it is not possible for us to extend further our Letter of Credit No. 2392, which expires on August 21. Please understand how serious and urgent it is for us to resolve this matter.
>
> We look forward to receiving your shipping advice, by fax, within the next seven days.
>
> Yours faithfully,
>
> [Signature]

b. Read the following letter and answer the questions.
- *Is the reply written in a direct way? Why?*
- *How many documents are there in the shipping documents? What is the certificate of guarantee?*

> Dear Sirs,
>
> Thank you for your letter of May 20 enquiring about the shipment of your order under Contract 8524. Please accept my apology for the delay which has been caused by the unavailability of shipping space from Bombay to London.
>
> Your consignment was shipped yesterday on board s. s. "Pandit" which is sailing directly to London.
>
> Enclosed please find one set of shipping documents comprising:
> - One non-negotiable copy of the bill of lading
> - Commercial invoice in duplicate
> - One copy of the certificate of guarantee
> - One copy of the certificate of quantity
> - One copy of the insurance policy
>
> I trust the goods will reach you in time for the winter selling season and prove to be entirely satisfactory. And I will personally ensure that you receive our prompt and careful attention at all times.
>
> Yours faithfully,
>
> [Signature]

8.1.2 Practice

A. Read and write a letter on Luisa Wang's behalf confirming the shipment terms agreed upon in the following conversation.

Lynette Smith: Can you ship the order within four or five weeks?
Luisa Wang: Five weeks, did you say?
Lynette Smith: Yes, four or five weeks. That's the shipping date from Shanghai, of course.
Luisa Wang: We could manage it in seven weeks.
Lynette Smith: Seven weeks? We can't wait that long.

Luisa Wang:	That's the best we can do just now, I'm afraid.
Lynette Smith:	Can't you make it six weeks?
Luisa Wang:	What about transshipment at Hong Kong? That would probably satisfy your demand of the shipment.
Lynette Smith:	As a rule, we don't give exporters permission to transship goods. As you know it adds to the risks of pilferage and damage.
Luisa Wang:	In that case, I'm afraid we can do very little about it.
Lynette Smith:	In order to ensure earlier shipment, we'd like to make this an exception and agree to transshipment.
Luisa Wang:	So we might as well mark "Transshipment at Hong Kong" in the contract.
Lynette Smith:	Agreed!

☞ **B. Read and comment on the following letter and then write a reply, making shipping advice.**

Dear Sirs,

　　We are very anxious to know about the shipment of our Order No. 538 for five metric tons of processed polyethylene for which we sent you about a month ago an irrevocable credit-expiration date being May 20.

　　As the selling season is rapidly approaching, our buyers are in urgent need of the goods. As the contracted time of delivery is rapidly falling due, it is imperative that you inform us of the delivery time and effect shipment as soon as possible.

　　Please expedite the execution of the order within the time stipulated, as any delay would cause us no little inconvenience and naturally financial loss.

　　We thank you very much for your immediate effectuation of the shipment.

Sincerely yours,
[Signature]

8.1.3　Case study & practice

　　Read and rearrange the numbered sentences in the right order. And then write a reply to confirm receiving the above letter.

Dear Sirs,

　　① The goods will reach you in time and turn out to your entire satisfaction.

　　② Enclosed you will find copies of relative shipping documents, so that you may make all the necessary preparations and find no difficulty in taking delivery of the goods when they arrive at your port.

　　③ We're pleased to inform you that your Order No. 336 of February 10 has now been completed and taken on board s.s. "Dongfeng" which, we are informed, will be sailing tomorrow.

Sincerely yours,
[Signature]

8.2 Communicating & Writing Skills

A. Read the following letter and learn how to negotiate about means of shipment.

Dear Mr Brown,

Thank you for your e-mail of July 15 that booked an order for three Model 880 machines. Our confirmation of order will be forwarded to you in two days.

Since the purchase is made on FOB basis, you are to ship the goods from Dalian on a liner to be designated by us. As soon as the shipping space is booked, we shall advise you of the name of the liner, on which the goods are to be shipped. For further instructions, please contact our forwarding agents, Phoenix International, Dalian Branch, who have hitherto taken care of the shipment for you and will contact you immediately.

As some parts of the machines are susceptible to shock, the machines must be packed in seaworthy cases capable of withstanding rough handling. The bright metal parts should be protected from water and dampness in transit.

Whether you are satisfied with this arrangement, or if you want us to help in any other way, please let us know.

Sincerely yours,

Jack Li

Study the following examples.

1) Because of the type of merchandise, we can only ship by truck (rail, etc.).
2) If the customer wishes to choose a carrier other than truck, he must bear the additional charges.
3) What connections do you have with shipping companies capable of handling a full charter? We need a ship of approximately 100,000 g.r.t. (gross registered tons).
4) Instead of s.s. Manhattan Maru as previously advised, you are now required to ship the goods of this order by s.s. CALCHAS.
5) To ensure fastest delivery, you are requested to forward the above order by air freight.

B. Read the following letter and learn how to urge arrangement of shipment.

Dear Sirs,

Re: Sales Confirmation No. B428

Thank you for your e-mail of yesterday.

We are pleased to tell you that the sample for 1 ×20′ FCL China Black Tea Standard No. B5432 under Sales Confirmation No. B428 has been approved by our end-user who is one of the largest tea buyers in Europe. Please ship the goods to Antwerp via Maersk as soon as possible.

When the shipment is effected, please advise us of the name of vessel, voyage number, container number and seal number, ETD and ETA immediately.

> Besides, please give special care to the quality and packing of the ordered goods. We trust that this order will lead to further business between us.
>
> Yours truly,
>
> [Signature]

Complete the following sentences by translating the parts in the brackets.

1) The above order is urgently needed. Therefore, we must _____ _____ (坚持快速装运).

2) _____ (要求马上交货).

3) Our order of leather shoes, _____ (应在6月交货), is now considerably overdue.

4) As the goods are urgently needed, could you _____ (请发货,不要再耽搁)?

5) Please let us know by fax _____ (我们什么时候可以收到货).

☞ **C. Read the following letter and learn how to advise shipment and sending of shipping documents.**

> Dear Mr Wood,
>
> The goods of 4,500 strands of wool you ordered May 28 were shipped this morning according to the stipulation set forth in the captioned L/C No. 996.
>
> The following copies of shipping documents are enclosed so that you may find no trouble in taking delivery of the goods when they arrive:
>
> Invoice No. 36 in duplicate
>
> Packing List No. 43 in duplicate
>
> Non-negotiable Bill of Lading No. PW790
>
> Insurance Policy No. HK453
>
> Survey Report No. SR576
>
> We hope the goods will arrive at the destination in perfect condition and appreciate very much your cooperation. We look forward to more cooperation between us in the future.
>
> Sincerely yours,
>
> Eric Luo

Fill in the blanks of the following sentences by using the appropriate forms of the word "ship".

1) We have the pleasure to inform you that the _____ per s.s. "Princess" has gone forward and hope that it will arrive at the destination in perfect condition.

2) The cargo has been _____ on s.s. "Qingdao" for transshipment at Hong Kong into s.s. "Princess".

3) The first lot under our Sales Confirmation No. 2691 will be _____ per s.s. "Nanfang" scheduled to sail on or about November 5.

4) We are pleased to inform you that we have booked _____ space for our Order No. 8975 of Chemical Fertilizer on s.s. "Daqing", ETA 15th May. For delivery instructions, please contact Lambard Bros. Co., Liverpool.

5) Having _____ the goods called for in Sales Confirmation No. 68932 by s.s. "Yunda", we send you herewith copies of the relative shipping documents comprising the following: ...

6) We are pleased to inform you that the first lot of 4,000 metric tons of soybeans under L/C No. 3682 has gone off on s.s. "Tung Feng", which sailed on July 7 for New York. Enclosed please find one set of the _____ documents.

D. Read the following letter and learn how to express one's inability to ship the goods on time.

Dear Sirs,

We thank you for your Letter of Credit No. E 102 amounting to USD 1,050,000 issued in our favor through the Hong Kong & Shanghai Banking Corporation.

With regard to shipment, we regret very much to inform you that despite strenuous efforts having been made by us, we are still unable to book space of a vessel sailing to Jakarta direct. The shipping companies here told us that, for the time being, there is no regular boat sailing between ports in China and Jakarta. Therefore, it is very difficult, if not impossible, for us to ship the 10,000 metric tons of sugar to Jakarta direct.

In view of the difficult situation faced by us, you are requested to amend the L/C to allow transshipment of the goods in Hong Kong where arrangements can easily be made for transshipment. Please be assured that we will ship the goods to Hong Kong right upon receipt of the L/C amendment. And your understanding of our position will be highly appreciated.

We are anxiously awaiting the amendment to the L/C.

Faithfully yours,
[Signature]

Write something in the following situations.

1) Tell the importer that you cannot effect shipment before the date named because your manufacturers are heavily committed.

2) Say that shipment cannot be effected as stipulated because the L/C does not arrive on time.

3) Tell the buyer that the shipment cannot be effected in the time limit of your credit because the mills have met with unforseen difficulties.

4) Say that goods can only be shipped next month because the only direct steamer which calls at your port once a month has just departed.

5) Tell the importer that the goods cannot be shipped in time as contracted and should be postponed to September and October owing to the delay in the opening of the covering L/C.

8.3 Writers' Workshop: Principles for BE Writing

Three Functions

Generally speaking, the functions of business writing are: 1) to inform, 2) to influence, and 3) to entertain. And the purpose of BE writing is to provide information and to make persuasion in expository writings such as business letters, reports, and contracts. BE writing which aims to inform is based upon facts and, BE writing which aims to persuade ought to give a certain clear point of view which is supported by facts. Only by giving enough clear information and by making convincing persuasion can you achieve the purpose of successful communication.

Six C's of BE Writing

In order to perform the functions of status enquiries, traders asking for information must remember that they are asking for a favor and therefore should write in polite and appreciative terms. When the information is received, no matter whether it is favorable or unfavorable, a suitable letter of acknowledgement and thanks must be sent. This is no more than common courtesy. In addition to the principle of courtesy, you should observe the following writing principles:

- *Conciseness*: In their book, *Teaching Business English*, Mark Ellis and Christine Johnson (1994: 9) said, "There is often a need to be concise—particularly when communicating by fax or telephone ... " In a business message every word counts and every sentence carries the message. Business people receive many messages every day. If you overburden them with unduly long expressions and tire their eyes with excess words, they might just toss your message in the nearby wastebasket.
- *Completeness*: Completeness refers to providing enough information so that the intention of the message is understood by the reader.
- *Correctness*: Correctness does not only mean using standard grammar and spelling, but it also means choosing suitable format for the situation and using language that is appropriate to the purpose of writing. Using appropriate language to the purpose of writing means choosing the exact words, selecting the appropriate sentence structures and creating careful paragraphs.
- *Concreteness*: Business writing ought to be vivid, specific and definite rather than vague, general and abstract, especially when the writer is requiring a response, solving a problem, making an offer or acceptance, etc. To make your message concrete, you can make use of facts and figures. And you can choose nouns and verbs with definite meanings.
- *Clarity*: Clarity is achieved through natural forms of expression, the use of familiar words and the logical arrangement of subject-matter. In business letter-writing and report-writing the language used should be as natural as the language of good everyday speech, but without its colloquialisms and slangs.
- *Courtesy*: Business message ought to show courteousness. People respond positively to those who treat them with respect and kindness. Nothing can take the place of words like "please" and "thank you". It should be remembered, however, that true courtesy requires more than the use of polite words and phrases. For instance, timely information with the desire to be helpful

and useful is a genuinely courteous message. When a letter cannot be answered promptly, for example, the information requested cannot be quickly obtained, it should be acknowledged immediately.

8.3.1 Group work

Work in groups of three or four and trying to find the problems with the following sentences. Then group the sentences with the same problem together and make improvement on them.

1) I wish to express my heartfelt gratitude to you for your kind cooperation.
2) All sales representatives will meet at 9:00 on Monday.
3) The Universal Trading Company is one of our big buyers.
4) Please be advised that we have received your invoice No. 264.
5) We have begun to export our machines to the foreign countries.
6) We hope to receive your catalogue by return mail. Thanking you in advance.
7) We wish to confirm our fax dispatched yesterday.
8) Mr Smith wrote to Mr Wang that he had received his order.
9) As to the steamer sailing from Shanghai to Los Angeles, we have bimonthly direct services.
10) We are sorry that you misunderstood us.

8.3.2 Comparing and commenting on the two complaint letters

Original Letter:

Dear Mr Wallace,

We can not regret too much when we consider the fact that this is the third time that deliveries have been made to our dissatisfaction. This is quite bad and unlike you in your usual mode of business, and we must request you to take immediate action to rectify this problem.

As a case in point, in our last order, only three bolts of the Lot 24 Linen (order A-445) were shipped when in fact five bolts were requested.

We hope you give this your immediate attention and take action to avoid such problems in the future.

Thank you in advance for your due settlement.

Sincerely yours,

Joyce Yeung

Revised Letter:

Dear Mr Wallace,

We ordered five bolts of Lot 24 Linen (Order No. A-445), but we received only three bolts. Would you please send the remaining two bolts immediately?

Incidentally, this is the third time that deliveries have been made in error. Is there anything wrong?

We are afraid that if these problems continue there will be trouble with our customers, so please do your best to correct the situation.

Also, may we have your comments?

Sincerely,

Joyce Yeung

8.3.3 Comment and improvement

Comment on the following letter which fails to follow some of the writing principles and see what improvement you can make.

Dear Denny, Clarice, Fouad, Rachel, and Mike,

As you have been apprised, we've been aware for some time that some of your people are punching in and out on the time clock for their friends, which leads to the end result that we pay these individuals for time they don't actually work. In spite of the fact that stern warnings about such dishonesty were issued along with requests that employees cooperate together to end the illegal practice, in many instances the practice continued on.

In staff meetings, you formulated a recommendation that we replace our current time clocks with a newer style that reads employees' palm prints because they cannot be utilized in a dishonest fashion. Yesterday, an executive decision was made in favour of that option.

At this point in time, you don't need to take any action, owing to the fact that we are in the stage of early advance planning to set the parameters of our needs. After we get bids on a new system, your feedback will be required.

Do not advise any of the employees about this upcoming change, because such statements might have an adverse effect in that they could possibly see this as their last opportunity to cheat.

The policy of firing everyone for cause who can be proved to have punched in and out for someone else or to have had his card punched in or out by someone else continues.

Regards,

[Signature]

Unit 9 Packing & Replies

Learning Objectives
- ✓ learning about packing and shipping marks
- ✓ learning how to negotiate about packing
- ✓ learning how to perform relative functions of language and communication
- ✓ learning how to write concretely

Identify Problems in the Following Writing & Comment

Dear Amada Levis,

    We write to advise you that we have today packed and shipped a consignment of garments on board of MV Pacific Centaur. The ship will sail from Dalian on April 21 and is due in San Francisco on May 10.

    We have the garments well packed and properly marked on every case so that you can have easy time when taking delivery.

    We have sent a full set of clean on board shipping company's B/L in triplicate, endorsed and marked as per instructions, together with certificate of origin, invoice (4 copies) and insurance certificate (2 copies) to Bank of China. I believe they can forward them to First California Commercial Bank in Los Angeles for payment.

    We trust we have done everything to facilitate the transaction for you.

Yours faithfully,
Allison Hu

9.1 Experience & Practice

9.1.1 Learning about packing and shipping marks

☞ **A. Brief introduction**

Questions: *What is packing in international trade? And what are the shipping marks in packing?*

    ① Packing

    Packing needs more care in foreign trade than in home trade. The real art of packing is to get the contents into a nice, compact shape that will stay that way during the roughest journey. Every buyer expects that his goods will reach him in perfect condition. Nothing is more annoying to a buyer than to find his goods damaged or part of his goods missing/lost on arrival. The seller must try to pack the goods in such a way that they will go through the ordeal of transport unscathed. It has been estimated that 70% of all cargo loss could be prevented by proper packaging and marking. There are two forms of packing: large/outer packing for transportation (transport packing) and small/inner packing for sales (sales packing).

Transport packing can protect commodity and help to transport, carry and store up. Sales packing should fit into the overall marketing concept, especially for consumer goods and industrial products to reinforce the corporate image with the customers. Thus, inner packing is for the purpose of drawing customers and fostering sales and plays the role of "a silent salesman". Therefore, it should be creative, elegant and attractive. Still, there is another type of packing, known as "neutral packing", which carries no mark of the name of the origin country and no sign of the original trademark, with a view to eluding the tariff of the import country or satisfying the importer's special requirements. On the whole, packing for transit has to strike a balance between two considerations: 1) It must be strong, safe, reliable and convenient enough to stand transportation hazards, to reduce the risk of goods being damaged in transit, to facilitate loading, unloading and stowage, and to prevent pilferage; 2) It must be as light and compact as possible to keep freight low.

② Shipping Marks in Packing

Shipping marks include the consignor's or consignee's code name, the number of the contract or the L/C, the port of destination and numbers of the packed goods. Directive marks are special instructions concerning proper manner of handling, storing, loading, lifting and unloading of the packed goods. Warning marks are various symbols and words stenciled on the packed goods to warn people against the hidden danger of inflammables, explosives and poisonous products.

③ Points to Remember

When you write letters concerning packing, you ought to follow the steps below:

- Open with some necessary information about the goods and with a statement, usually about packing.
- Give information about the packing methods.
- Expect an answer to the packing instructions.

☞ **B. Experience by reading and answering questions.**

a. Read the following letter and answer the questions.
- *What does the writer instruct about in the letter?*
- *Are the instructions specific and clear?*

Dear Sirs,

We are pleased to tell you that the bed sheets you shipped have arrived here in perfect condition, which shows that you have made considerable improvement in packing.

As for the 1,000 dozen sets of your pillowcases to be shipped to us, we suggest you have them packed each in a polybag, half dozen to a box and 10 dozens to a wooden case. Furthermore, we should like you to have the fiber content label sewn to the outside of the pillowcase instead of to the inside as your sample shows. The customs regulations require that the label be visible from the outside. We believe that you will pay special attention to the packing so as to avoid any damage in transit or inconvenience in going through the customs formalities.

Please let us know whether these requirements can be met.

Sincerely yours,

[Signature]

b. Read the following letter and answer the questions.
- *How is the reply written? Direct or indirect?*
- *Are the inquiries about the packing specific and concrete?*

Gentlemen,

Thank you for your proposal of October 20 for the packing manner of the goods under our Order No. 968. Our clients wish to know the particulars of packing of your embroidered blouse, namely,
- ♦ In what manner will the goods be packed so that the packing looks attractive and helpful to the sales?
- ♦ What effective measures will you take to prevent the goods from dampness or rain?
- ♦ What kind of packing materials will be used to make the packing strong enough to withstand rough handling, prevent the goods from damage or pilferage, and make it comparatively convenient to handle in the course of loading and unloading?
- ♦ What steps will you take to ensure that the inner packing will not be torn apart?

We look forward to receiving from you any information concerning the above by return.

Sincerely yours,

[Signature]

9.1.2 Practice

A. Read the following conversation and on Mr Zhang's behalf, write a letter confirming the packing terms agreed upon in the following conversation.

Mr Reading: Mr Zhang, shall we discuss the packing now?

Mr Zhang: All right. As to towels, we pack them 10 dozens to one carton, gross weight around 20 kilos a carton.

Mr Reading: Cartons?

Mr Zhang: Yes, corrugated cardboard boxes.

Mr Reading: I'm afraid cartons are not strong enough for such a heavy load.

Mr Zhang: The cartons are comparatively light and therefore easy to handle. Besides,

	we'll reenforce the cartons with double straps.
Mr Reading:	Maybe you are right. But the packing should be suitable for transport by sea. You know the goods are to be transshipped at Hong Kong.
Mr Zhang:	You needn't worry about that. So far, no customers have complained about our packing.
Mr Reading:	OK. Am I to understand the packing in cartons reenforced with double straps and lined with plastic sheets?
Mr Zhang:	Exactly.
Mr Reading:	Very good. We have successfully settled the problem of packing. I'll open the L/C immediately after I return to Bombay.
Mr Zhang:	All right. We'll make the shipment as soon as your L/C is available.

☞ **B. Read the following letter and write a reply, negotiating about packing terms.**

Dear Mr Green,

We hereby inform you that for your future order for our ready-made clothes we shall recommend packing them in cartons rather than in wooden cases, as carton packing possesses the following advantages:

◇ Packing in cartons will help prevent skillful pilferage since the traces of pilferage will be more evident.

◇ Packing in cartons is an extensively used and fairly fit mode of packing for ocean transportation.

◇ Our cartons are well protected against moisture by plastic lining. As they are made of paperboard, special attention is paid in handling and storage.

◇ Our cartons are comparatively light and compact, so they are more convenient and safer to handle.

The above comments are on the basis of a comparative study and analysis of the advantages and disadvantages of the two packing modes, i.e. packing in cartons and packing in wooden cases, as well as the results of shipments already made. Of course, occasional accidents in peculiar cases are inevitable, as it is with packing in wooden cases. It is believed, however, that as long as we cooperate closely with each other, you will find our improvement in carton packing satisfactory.

It will be highly appreciated if you can inform us of your further comments at an early date.

Sincerely yours,

John Watson

9.1.3 Case study & practice

☞ **A. Read the following letter and fill in the blanks.**

June 3, 2020

Dear Sirs,

Thank you ____①____ your letter ____②____ May 20, 2020 and we confirm that we are still offering our range ____③____ luxury foods ____④____ the prices quoted ____⑤____ our initial offer

106　A Coursebook for Business English Writing

> ____⑥____ you.
>   We understand your concern ____⑦____ packing and assure you that we take every possible precaution to ensure that our products reach our customers all over the world ____⑧____ prime condition.
>   ____⑨____ your information, "Ariel" caviar is packed as follows:
>   Each jar is wrapped ____⑩____ tissue paper ____⑪____ being placed in its individual decorative cardboard box. The boxes are then packed ____⑫____ strong cardboard cartons, twelve ____⑬____ a carton, separated ____⑭____ each other ____⑮____ corrugated paper dividers.
>   The cartons are then packed ____⑯____ strong wooden crates. Since the crates are specially made to hold twenty-four cartons, there is no danger ____⑰____ movement ____⑱____ them. In addition, the crates are lined ____⑲____ waterproof, airtight material. The lids are secured ____⑳____ nailing, and the crates are strapped ____㉑____ metal bands.
>   In the case of consignments being sent to you, transshipment at Buenos Aires will be necessary, so each case will be marked with details required by the Argentinian authorities, as well as with your own mark, details of weight, etc., and symbols representing the following warnings and directions:
>   USE NO HOOKS! STOW AWAY FROM HEAT! THIS SIDE UP, and DO NOT DROP.
>   You will be completely satisfied with our answer to your questions, and we are looking forward to receiving orders from you.
>   Yours sincerely,
>   [Signature]

☞ **B. Read the above letter and write a reply saying that you are completely satisfied with the seller's cooperation.**

9.2　Communicating & Writing Skills

☞ **A. Read the following letter and learn how to make instructions about packing.**

> Dear Mr Watkins,
>   Thank you for your letter of February 12. We are glad to tell you that we have opened an irrevocable L/C this morning with the Standard Chartered Bank here for 1,200 kilograms of tea. The required shipping space has been booked on s.s. "East Wind" due to sail from Shanghai to our port at the end of next month. Please try your best to have the goods ready and ship them by that vessel without any delay.
>   Regarding packing, the tea should be packed in polybags of 500 grams each, 5 polybags to a tea box, 24 boxes on a pallet and 50 pallets in an FCL container with our shipping marks on the outer packing.
>   We trust the above is clear to you and look forward to your shipping advice.
>   Yours sincerely,
>   Michael Lee

Study the following examples.

1) There is a good deal of advantage in attractive packing.
2) A packing that catches the eye will help us push the sales.
3) Packing also affects the reputation of our products.
4) I'm sure the new packing will give your clients satisfaction.
5) We advocate the use of smaller containers.
6) Compact packing has much merit (many merits).
7) We are of the opinion that improvement in packaging will push sales a long way forward.
8) Buyers take up the position that the seeds must be packed in double bags.

☞ **B. Read the following letter and learn how to make instructions about shipping marks in packing.**

Dear Sirs,

With reference to the shipment of our Order No. 5688 for 200 cases of china wares, we wish to draw your attention to the following:

As the goods are susceptible to be broken, the wares must be packed in seaworthy cases capable of withstanding rough handling.

Please mark the cases with our initials in a diamond, under which comes the destination with contract number and stencil conspicuously the words: "FRAGILE, HANDLE WITH CARE" on both sides of the cases.

We trust that the above instructions are clear to you and look forward to your reply.

Yours faithfully,
[Signature]

Translate the following sentences into English.

1) 货物应标上我方缩写名称,外加菱形(圆形、三角形等)。
2) 箱(盒、袋、桶等)上请按照所给图样加上标志。
3) 除非你方另有通知,我们将仍在货包上刷以前的标志。
4) 包装上必须标以不易磨掉的唛头。
5) 在外包装上请标明"小心轻放"字样。

☞ **C. Read the following letters and learn how to negotiate about packing problems and their settlement.**

⊕ **A letter complaining about packing**

Dear Sirs,

A shipment of ready-made garments arrived on July 10. Having examined the goods thoroughly, we have found that the packing needs improvement. For instance, the cartons used are not strong enough to protect the contents from getting damaged during transit. We have enquired some of our clients about the packing in question. Their answers are summed up as follows:

- Such cartons are easy to cut open because the cardboard of which the cartons are made is rather thin, thus making pilferage possible.
- If and when the goods are to be transshipped at a certain port, the cartons will stand in the open on the wharf and, in heavy rains, be subjected to damage as the cartons will surely be soaked.
- During loading and unloading, the cartons are to be piled up; hence breakage is unavoidable because the cartons are too thin to stand heavy pressure.
- The insurance companies, on knowing this, will shift their responsibilities to the goods being packed in cartons not fit for ocean transportation and refuse compensation for losses.

From the above comments, you can readily see that our clients are justified in their anxieties over your packing. As far as packing is concerned, they prefer wooden cases to cartons for future shipments. Please consider the above problem seriously and make improvements on the packing.

Looking forward to your early reply.

Yours sincerely,

[Signature]

⊕ Reply to the letter concerning packing problem

Dear Sirs,

Thank you for your letter of July 16, informing us of your clients' comments on our packing. We have discussed the matter with the competent department here and wish to explain as follows:

- The cartons we use are up to standard and fit for ocean transportation. For years we have used these cartons in our shipments to many continental ports to the entire satisfaction of our clients. Moreover, the insurance companies have accepted such packing for WPA and TPND.
- These cartons are well protected against moisture by plastic lining. Thus garments packed in them are not so susceptible to damage by moisture as packed in wooden cases.
- The cardboard used for making cartons is light but compact. It keeps down packaging costs and helps customers save on freight.
- Your clients' anxieties over packing are presumed. We are confident that the insurance company can be made to pay the necessary compensation for any loss or losses from pilferage and breakage caused by using such cartons.

Please tell your clients that their fears are unwarranted. Nowadays, except for bulk cargo, nude cargo and huge machinery, most commodities are packed in cartons. To pack garments in wooden cases is obsolete. For future shipments, we are experimenting with special cartons, in which garments are hung on dresshangers. These cartons can be containerized, so that the garments will not twist.

We highly value your comments and assure you of our cooperation.

Yours sincerely,

[Signature]

Complete the following sentences by translating the parts in brackets into English.

1) The quality is quite nice, _____ (但包装完全不能吸引买主).

2) Buyers have made a complaint for _____ (不良包装).

3) The shipment arrived _____ （情况不佳，许多袋子破损渗漏）.
4) We have already taken steps to _____ （改进包装）and are confident that our future shipments will give you complete satisfaction.
5) As the steamer sails next Monday, we _____ （没有时间改变包装）.

9.3 Writers' Workshop: Concreteness vs Abstractness

Concreteness vs Abstractness

Concreteness and abstractness are two opposite requirements for writing and qualities for rhetoric. These two qualities are required on different occasions for different purposes. Where and when to prefer one of them just depends.

On most occasions you are required to be concrete in your wording, especially in BE practical writing. To achieve the purpose of being concrete or specific, you had better make use of specific figures and words with specific denotations. For example, it is better to set forth the exact date for shipment or delivery than to give vague expressions such as "prompt shipment" and "immediate delivery". For other purposes, however, you might have to write in words and terms with abstract and general meanings rather than in specific or concrete ones. One of the purposes is that you just leave enough room for others to express their ideas. Please note the underlined words or terms with abstract meaning in the following example.

Although we are interested in your products, we find your price is so high that our margin of profit would be either very little or nil. As you probably know, the socks available at present on the market manufactured by several Hong Kong factories are of superior quality and the price is 10%–15% lower than yours. We hope, therefore, you will reduce your price so as to stand up to the competition.

9.3.1 Group work

Work in groups of three or four and try to rewrite the following sentences in concrete and specific terms.

1) We will amend the L/C as soon as possible.
2) We wish to confirm our fax dispatched yesterday.
3) We will deliver your things soon.
4) Your new, lightweight Electro Shredder can easily be carried from room to room.
5) The majority of our stockbrokers voted for the new plan.
6) Your savings account will earn high interest.
7) You will receive your refund cheque soon.

9.3.2 Reading and completing the following letter according to the Chinese given in the brackets

Dear Sirs,

　　With reference to ＿＿＿＿①＿＿＿＿（6月27日来函）, we are glad to learn that you wish to enter into trade relations with us, which also meets our interest.

　　We are, at present, very much interested in ＿＿＿＿②＿＿＿＿（进口你方瓷器）and would appreciate your sending us ＿＿＿＿③＿＿＿＿（产品目录、样品册）or even samples if possible.

　　Please give us detailed information of CIF prices, ＿＿＿＿④＿＿＿＿（折扣及付款条件）.

　　We hope this will be a good start for a long and profitable business relation.

　　　　　　　　　　　　　　　　　　　　　　　　　　Yours faithfully,
　　　　　　　　　　　　　　　　　　　　　　　　　　[Signature]

9.3.3 Comment and improvement

Comment on the following letter which fails to follow the writing principle of being concrete and see what improvement you can make.

To: Public Relations Staff
From: Al Nantz
Re: Promotion

　　Resheba Jones has been promoted to the position of senior trade show manager from her current position as a manager. She will run our in-house trade show department and report directly to me. Trade show department managers and associates will report to Resheba. All national and international shows will be planned and managed by her. She will also attend the regional shows, overseeing on-site set-ups and post-show teardowns of booths of 4,000 square feet and larger. At the same time that she is super-visiting a trade show booth, she will maintain long-distance management of other shows. Internally, she will manage special events and incentive programs.

　　Let's make a point of congratulating Resheba on this significant recognition of her hard work and abilities.

Unit 10 Insurance & Replies

Learning Objectives

✓ learning about insurance of the goods
✓ learning how to negotiate about international insurance
✓ learning how to perform relative functions of language and communication
✓ learning about the qualities of effective sentence writing

Identify Problems in the Following Writing & Comment

Dear Sir or Madam,

　　Your company has been introduced to us by one of our business partners as a prospective purchaser of china, this item comes within our range of operations, so we shall be pleased to enter into business relations with you at an early date.

　　To give you a general idea of the various kinds of china now available for export, we are enclosing a brochure and a price list, quotations and samples will be airmailed to you after receiving your specific enquiry, and we are looking forward to your early reply.

Yours sincerely,
Hans Seitz

10.1　Experience & Practice

10.1.1　Learning about insurance of the goods

☞ **A. Brief introduction**

Questions: *How much do you know about insurance? What are the basic types of insurance provided by the PICC?*

　　① Insurance of the Goods

　　If a transaction is concluded on a CIF basis, the exporter should, before or after effecting shipment, notify the importer of their dispatch. In case of CFR transaction, a shipping advice is necessary for the importer to cover insurance of the relevant goods.

　　Goods are always insured in transit through an insurance company or insurance broker. In international trade, transportation of goods from the seller to the buyer usually covers a long distance by sea, by land or by air, and has to go through the procedures of loading, unloading and storing. During this process it is quite possible that the goods will encounter various kinds of perils and sometimes suffer losses.

Claims for damage or loss may be made if the goods have been damaged, lost or interfered within transit. When a consignment is received, it is examined and the delivery note is signed to confirm that the goods have been received and that they are damaged if they should be. However, damage and errors are often noticed later when the container or the package is unpacked and rechecked. It is customary to employ brokers not only for the conclusion of a contract of insurance but also for the settlement of claims. If the consignee is informed that the goods have arrived damaged, he should immediately notify the insurer's agent at the port of discharge who will survey the goods and issue a survey report. Then he could claim indemnity from the insurer by producing the insurance policy, survey report and other necessary documents.

② The Insurance Policy

The basic instrument in insurance is the policy. A policy is a contract, a legal document, and its principal function is to serve as evidence of the agreement between the insurer and the assured. A policy must be produced to lodge a claim in court of law (but not against insurers).

③ Insurance Coverage

Insurance coverage varies in extent. The People's Insurance Company of China (PICC) provides three basic types: Free from Particular Average (F.P.A.), With Particular Average (W.P.A.) and All Risks. Besides, it provides other extraneous risks which are divided into two groups, General Additional Risk including TPND, Freshwater and/or Rain Damage, Risk of Shortage, Risk of Intermixture and Contamination, etc.; Special and Specific Additional Risk including Failure to Deliver, Import Duty Risk, On Deck Risk, Rejection Risk, Aflatoxin Risk, War Risk, Strikes Risk, etc.

④ Points to Remember

When you write about insurance, you ought to follow the steps below:
- Open with reference to some necessary information about the deal, or open with a statement about insurance.
- Give information about the insurance arrangement.
- End with goodwill.

B. Experience by reading and answering questions.

a. Read the following letter and answer the questions.
- *What does the writer instruct about in the letter?*
- *What hope does the writer express in the closing of the letter?*

Unit 10　Insurance & Replies　113

Dear Sirs,

　　We refer to our Order No. 353 for 400 sets of sewing machines, from which you will see that this order is placed on a CFR basis.

　　As we now desire to have the shipment insured at your end, please arrange to insure the goods on our behalf against All Risks at the invoice value plus 10%, i. e. US $5,400.00.

　　We shall of course refund the premium to you upon receipt of your debit note or, if you like, you may draw on us at sight for the amount required.

　　We sincerely hope that our request will meet with your approval.

Yours sincerely,

[Signature]

b. Read the following letter and answer the questions.
- *What kind of letter is the following one? How is the letter?*
- *Does the writer make the shipping advice in the closing of the letter?*

Dear Sirs,

　　We have recieved your May 23 letter asking us to effect insurance on the goods for your account.

　　For transactions concluded on CFR basis, our usual practice is to cover All Risks for 110% of the invoice value up to the port of destination. At your request, we are taking out insurance on your behalf with the People's Insurance Company of China and, the policy is being prepared accordingly and will be sent to you by the end of the month together with our debit note for the premium.

　　For your information, we are arranging to ship the goods by m. v. "Qingdao" scheduled to sail on or about June 10.

Yours sincerely,

[Signature]

10.1.2　Practice

A. Read the following conversation and on Mr Smith's behalf, write a letter of arranging insurance on its basis.

Mr Smith:　　Good morning, I'm John Smith, an Australian businessman and I'm here today to look for insurance from your company.

Mr Huang:　　Welcome to PICC. My name is Huang. Have a seat, please.

Mr Smith:　　Thank you, Mr Huang. First, I'd like to know what kind of insurance you can provide.

Mr Huang:　　Well, we are able to cover all kinds of risks for different means of transportation such as marine, land, air and parcel post as well.

Mr Smith:　　That's great! I have a batch of glass works to be shipped to Australia. Which risks do you recommend?

Mr Huang:　　We serve our clients with a wide range of coverage against all kinds of risks for sea transportation, such as F. P. A., W. P. A., All Risks and Additional Risks of course. You'd better make your decision after reading

114 A Coursebook for Business English Writing

	this leaflet.
Mr Smith:	OK, let me have a look. I think F. P. A. is enough. What do you think?
Mr Huang:	If I were you, I would arrange for W. P. A. plus additional coverage against Risk of Breakage and TPND. You see, your consignment is fragile as well as precious. So, they are more suitable.
Mr Smith:	Your suggestion sounds reasonable. Thank you.
Mr Huang:	My pleasure.

☞ **B. Read the following letter and complete the reply by translating the Chinese in the brackets.**

May 8, 2007

Dear Sirs,

　　Please ensure us against All Risks US $100,000.00 value of 5,000 sets of "Butterfly" Sewing Machines shipped at Shanghai, on board s. s. "Fengching", sailing for New York on May 20.

　　Please send us the policy, together with the debit note for the premium.

　　　　　　　　　　　　　　　　　　　　　　　　　　Yours sincerely,
　　　　　　　　　　　　　　　　　　　　　　　　　　[Signature]

Reply to the above letter

Dear Sirs,

　　Regarding your instructions of May 8, ＿＿＿＿＿＿①＿＿＿＿＿＿（我方已为你方运货投了险）of 5,000 sets of "Butterfly" Sewing Machines shipped from Shanghai on board s. s. "Fengching", sailing for New York on May 20, ＿＿＿＿＿＿②＿＿＿＿＿（如附寄的保单所示）.

　　Please ＿＿＿＿＿＿③＿＿＿＿＿＿（汇1 200美元到我账户）for this policy bank check.

　　　　　　　　　　　　　　　　　　　　　　　　　　Yours faithfully,
　　　　　　　　　　　　　　　　　　　　　　　　　　[Signature]

10.1.3　Case study & practice

☞ **A. Read the following letter and rearrange it in the right order.**

Dear Sirs,

　　① In particular we wish to know whether you can issue a special rate for the promise of regular monthly shipments.

　　② We regularly ship consignments of Maotai Jiu to Antwerp by both passenger and cargo liners of Far East Shipping Line.

　　③ Would you please say whether you can issue an all-risks policy for these shipments and if so, on what terms?

　　　　　　　　　　　　　　　　　　　　　　　　　　Yours sincerely,
　　　　　　　　　　　　　　　　　　　　　　　　　　[Signature]

☞ **B. Read the above letter and write a reply saying that you will give a special rate of 0.9% in view of regular monthly shipments.**

10.2 Communicating & Writing Skills

☞ **A. Read the following letters and learn how to ask for and about insurance of the goods.**

Letter 1

Dear Sirs,
　　We will make a shipment of 800 cases of toys by s. s. "Qianjin", due to leave for Los Angeles on November 14.
　　We intend to insure the consignment against All Risks at invoice value plus 10%, i. e. US $23,000.00 and thank you if you let us have the policy ASAP.

　　　　　　　　　　　　　　　　　　　　　　　　　　Yours faithfully,
　　　　　　　　　　　　　　　　　　　　　　　　　　[Signature]

Letter 2

Dear Sirs,
　　We shall recently have a consignment of raincoats under the Order No. 546 enclosed, valued at US $4,000 (four thousand US dollars only) CIF Hong Kong, to be shipped to Osaka by a vessel of Yokohama Liners Ltd.
　　We desire to have the shipment insured against All Risks from our warehouse at the above address to the port of Osaka. Will you please tell us the terms and conditions on which you can provide cover for the risks mentioned?
　　We look forward to the insurance policy.

　　　　　　　　　　　　　　　　　　　　　　　　　　Yours faithfully,
　　　　　　　　　　　　　　　　　　　　　　　　　　[Signature]

Fill in the blanks of the following sentences with the words given below.

　　cover　　effect　　insure　　insured　　coverage　　insurance

1) Please _____ us on the goods detailed below.
2) Please _____ insurance for my account of US $55,000 on my goods, against All Risks, from Hong Kong to this city, and at the lowest premium possible, not exceeding 10%.

3) Will you please arrange to _____ for us on the following consignment of crockery goods from our warehouse at the above address to Manila?

4) We desire to have the shipment _____ against All Risks from our warehouse at the above address to the port of Osaka.

5) W. P. A. is too narrow a coverage. Please _____ against all risks.

6) We want broader _____ including TPND.

7) _____ is to cover both sea (water-borne) and overland (road) transport.

B. Read the following letters and learn how to offer and accept the insurance rate.

⊕ **A letter offering the rate**

Dear Sirs,

Thank you for your letter of August 7 and we are pleased to note that you would like to insure with us a shipment of glassware from Tianjin to New York by sea.

The rate now being charged by us for the proposed shipment against All Risks including War Risk is 1% subject to our own Ocean Marine Cargo Clauses and Ocean Marine War Risk Clauses, copies of which are enclosed.

If you find our rate acceptable, please let us know the details of your shipment so that we may issue our policy accordingly.

We are looking forward to your early reply.

                 Yours faithfully,
                 [Signature]

⊕ **A letter saying to accept the rate**

Dear Sirs,

Thank you for your letter of July 20 informing us of your insurance rate.

We accept your rate of 0.412%. Please effect immediate insurance, ICC (B) including War Risk, at the rate quoted on the goods mentioned below:

600 toys, valued at US $33,000.00 going from London to Los Angeles by s.s. "Qianjin" sailing from London on December 12.

The goods are packed in black wooden cases.

We look forward to receiving the policy before the end of this month. Meanwhile, please confirm that you hold the goods covered.

                 Yours faithfully,
                 [Signature]

Translate the following sentences into English.

1) 这笔保险费是按所报 2 590 美元的货值的 0.65% 的保险费率收取。

2) 这批货价值 100 万美元。我们可以接受你们 0.45% 的保险费率。

3) 现奉告,根据我公司海洋运输货物保险条款和海洋运输货物战争险条款的规定,承保上述货物一切险包括战争险的现行费率是 1%。

☞ **C. Read the following letter and learn how to negotiate about payment of insurance.**

> Dear Mr Wen,
>
> We regret to inform you that the goods received for our Order No. 4832 have been found damaged by improper handling.
>
> We have arranged for insurance company's surveyor to investigate the damage and now enclose the report and the shipping agent's statement for your reference. As you hold the insurance policy we should be thankful if you would take the matter up for us with the insurance company.
>
> We hope no difficulty will arise in connection with the insurance claim and thank you in advance for your trouble on our behalf.
>
> Sincerely yours,
Ting Chole

Translate the following sentences into Chinese.
1) Responsibility lies with the insurance company.
2) This is purely an insurance case, with which we are not concerned.

10.3　Writers' Workshop: Qualities of Effective Sentence Writing

To acquire the qualities of effective sentences, sentences should be concise, coherent, and vivid to serve the purpose of modern communications.

Writing Concise Sentences

An effective sentence shouldn't contain unnecessary words. Ideas should be expressed with simple, clear words and expressions. Wordiness only obscures the idea, instead of clarifying it. A good writer usually prefers simple and clear expressions like "because" and "soon" to long and wordy ones like "due to the fact that" and "in the near future".

Writing Coherent Sentences

A sentence is coherent when its words are properly and logically connected, and their relationships should be unmistakably clear. Coherence is violated when the following problems arise:
- Sentence with dangling modifiers or misplaced modifiers
- Faulty parallel construction
- Run-on sentences and faulty comma

Avoiding Outdated Commercialese and Abused Passive Voice

Out-of-date commercialese makes business letters rigid and cold. And too many uses of the passive voice tend to be dull and impersonal in writing effect. Therefore, you should avoid the old-fashioned commercialese and try not to use the passive voice too much in order to make your writing as modern and forceful as possible.

10.3.1 Group work

Work in groups and try to make the following sentences simpler and more forceful.

1) American business has a goal, which is to try to raise the standard of living.
2) He is someone who has accomplished a great deal in a short period of time.
3) It is important to read the instructions before using the machine.
4) There are several pages in Mr Smith's report concerning budgeting.

10.3.2 Revising the following sentences to make them logical or structurally-balanced

1) To meet the technique requirement of the customer, a new method has been adopted in production.
2) Working as fast as possible, the budget soon was ready.
3) The president spoke with warmth and in a humorous way.
4) After a two-week slump, we increased the sales.

10.3.3 Comment and improvement

Make your comment before making improvement on the following letter in which the passive voice is abused.

Dear Mr Hall,

　　Please be advised that the above order should have been received by the end of January. Would you please let us know (right away) what the status is?

　　Your prompt reply would be highly appreciated.

　　　　　　　　　　　　　　　　　　　　　Sincerely yours,

　　　　　　　　　　　　　　　　　　　　　Peter Bentley

Unit 11　Claims & Adjustments

Learning Objectives

✓ learning about claims and adjustments
✓ learning how to negotiate about claims and adjustments
✓ learning how to perform relative functions of language and communication
✓ learning about the positive tone and "You"-attitude in writing

---

Identify Problems in the Following Writing & Comment

Dear Mr Wood,

　　Do you have a vacancy on your staff for an assistant accountant?

　　My education and experience give me the full confidence to apply for this position. I graduated from Dongbei University of Finance and Economics, majoring in accounting. I have been working in the costing department of ABC Company for the past two years. I think I am the best assistant accountant in that company. The only reason for my seeking another job is that ABC is not a place where I can bring my potential into full play. And I think your company is the best place for me.

　　Attached is my CV, together with the names of my references. If there is some opportunity of a vacancy occurring in the near future, I would greatly appreciate being given an interview.

　　I look forward to your reply.

Yours faithfully,
Lin Lin

11.1　Experience & Practice

11.1.1　Learning about claims and adjustments

☞ **A. Brief introduction**

Questions: *What might be the causes for complaints? And what rules are to be followed when dealing with complaints and claims?*

　　① Complaints and Claims

　　As you know, nothing goes as well as what is expected. Due to many unforeseen factors, errors sometimes occur, goods are mishandled, accidents happen, etc. All these may result in subsequent complaints and claims of different kinds. They might be as follows:

- complaint of wrong goods delivered;
- complaint of goods of inferior quality;
- complaint of shipment damaged, short, or missing;
- complaint of goods delayed or badly packed;
- complaint of mixed-up delivery;
- complaint of wrong-billed invoice;
- complaint of excessively-charged prices.

② How to Deal with Complaints and Claims

Regardless of the character of complaints and claims, the making of complaints or lodging of claims is an unpleasant matter and needs to be well prepared. Otherwise, business would become unprofitable and pointless, and future business relationships may be jeopardized.

Letters in reply to complaints or claims should always be courteous. Even if the complaint is unfounded, the seller should not say so until they have good and reliable grounds on which to repudiate the complaint.

③ Points to Remember

When something unpleasant should happen, you ought to write or communicate by following the points below:

- Complain or claim immediately. You should complain or claim without any hesitation or the least delay when you find out a defect, damage, deficiency or a delay in connection with your goods.
- Address the reader politely. Perhaps cutting loose with a loud and lusty complaint will relieve your frustration. However, always tear up any nasty letter you may write in a huff. Do not resort to sarcasm or name-calling. Make sure that your letter is polite and business-like.
- Explain the problem clearly by providing specific details. You should make it clear what your grievances are and what has failed to be done. Keep the letter short by deleting any narrative words and expressions.
- Make a specific request. Clearly spell out what action you want taken. Never leave it up to your reader to guess!
- Stronger terms may be used in your follow-up complaints if you fail to get a reply or a satisfactory correction from the reader within a reasonable time. Even this letter, however, should be addressed politely.

B. Experience by reading and answering questions.

a. Read the following letter and answer the questions.

- *What does the writer complain about in the letter?*
- *Is the writer direct in his complaint?*

Unit 11　Claims & Adjustments

Dear Sirs,

　　With reference to our Order No. 315, we are compelled to complain about the inferior quality. Compared to Sample No. 169, the obtained self-adhesive correction tape is very transparent and does not satisfactorily cover the error being corrected.

　　We would like to have your explanation of the inferiority in the quality, and also to know what you purpose to do in this matter.

　　　　　　　　　　　　　　　　　　　　　　　　Yours faithfully,
　　　　　　　　　　　　　　　　　　　　　　　　[Signature]

　　b. Read the following letter and answer the questions.
　　● *What kind of letter is the following one?*
　　● *What response does the writer make to the complaint?*

Dear Sirs,

　　We are sorry to learn that your order we sent you on March 25 arrived damaged. We shall grant you an allowance of 20% on the invoiced cost as you proposed. Please accept our sincere apology.

　　We hope the inconvenience to you is small and thank you for bringing this matter to our attention.

　　　　　　　　　　　　　　　　　　　　　　　　Sincerely yours,
　　　　　　　　　　　　　　　　　　　　　　　　[Signature]

11.1.2　Practice

A. Read the following conversation and on Mr Maxwell's behalf, write a letter on its basis making a complaint.

Mr Maxwell: The January shipment of sewing machines was found seriously damaged. I think you shall be responsible for the damage.

Mr Horner: We're very sorry for the damage, but you should lodge a claim against the insurance company.

Mr Maxwell: We did lodge a claim, but the insurance company refused it on the ground that the loss is out of the range of coverage.

Mr Horner: We only covered FPA on your behalf and are thus not responsible for the insurer's refusal.

Mr Maxwell: The insurer said that the damage was caused by improper packing and that we should file a claim against the seller.

Mr Horner: If that's the case, we'd like you to present the relevant certificate issued by an inspection organization acceptable to us.

Mr Maxwell: I've brought it with me. Here you are.

Mr Horner: We'll have a study of it first and let you know the results in two days.

☞ **B. Read the following letter and write a reply to it.**

Dear Sirs,

We have received the documents and taken delivery of the goods on arrival of s. s. "Eastwind" at Dalian.

Thank you for the prompt execution of the order. Everything appears to be correct and in good condition except in Case No. 32.

Unfortunately, when we opened Case No. 32, we found completely different items in it. We can only presume that a mistake was made and the contents of this case were for another order.

As we need the items we ordered to complete deliveries to our new customers, we must ask you to arrange for the despatch of replacements immediately. We attach a list of the contents of Case No. 32, and shall be glad if you will check this with our order and the copy of your invoice.

In the meantime we are holding the above-mentioned case at your disposal. Please let us know what you wish us to do with it.

Yours sincerely,
[Signature]

11.1.3 Case study & practice

Write a letter according to the given facts, claiming for the loss of **RMB 850 plus inspection fee**.

- The Survey Report from Shanghai Commodity Inspection Bureau evidences that all drums of apple juice weigh short by from 1 to 5 kilograms, totaling 300 kilograms.
- The apple juice was short weight before shipment as the drums were intact.
- You are enclosing the Survey Report No. TE115 and looking forward to settlement at an early date.

11.2 Communicating & Writing Skills

☞ **A. Read the following letter and learn how to make complaints.**

Dear Sirs,

<u>Re: Claim on Wool Carpet</u>

The captioned goods you shipped per s. s. "Peace" on March 2 arrived here yesterday.

On examination, nearly 20% of the packages had been broken and the carpets were in the open. It was obviously attributed to improper packing.

We are, therefore, compelled to claim on you to compensate us for the loss, US $1,000.00 which we have sustained by the damage to the goods. We should like to take this opportunity to suggest that special care be taken in your future deliveries.

We are awaiting your early reply.

Yours sincerely,
[Signature]

Complete the following sentences by translating the Chinese in the brackets.

1) We would like to know what you propose to do in the matter, as _____ _____（它们达不到我们的目的，我们不能使用）.

2) Since it is agreed that we have the right to reject the goods when they are _____ _____（不合质量要求）upon examination by China Commodity Inspection Bureau at the port of destination, we regret to inform you that we have to _____ _____（把货退给你们，费用由你们负担）.

3) The outcome of the shipment is not satisfactory, as is _____ _____（由中国商检局证明）.

4) We duly received the 15 cases of Menthol Crystals you sent us, but regret to say that on examination, five of them were found to _____（严重受损）, _____（明显是由包装不当所致）.

5) We examined them one by one and found that each of them was _____ _____（多多少少有些渗漏）.

☞ **B. Read the following letter and learn how to lodge a claim.**

Dear Sirs,

　　We have received your shipment covering our Order No. 2122 for 200 units of electric heater, which you shipped by M/S "President". But much to our regret, we have to inform you that we have found that one of the cases of your consignment is in a badly damaged condition. Among the goods, the panels of 20 heaters were broken and the mechanisms were exposed. It looks as if some heavy cargo had fallen on it.

　　As you see in our survey report stating twenty sets of heaters severely damaged, these goods are quite unsaleable. Therefore, we would ask you to ship replacements for the broken goods as soon as possible while we will register our claim with the insurance company. We hope the matter will come to your best attention.

　　　　　　　　　　　　　　　　　　　　　　　　　　　Yours faithfully,
　　　　　　　　　　　　　　　　　　　　　　　　　　　[Signature]

Study the examples.

1) We have to claim on you for US $500.

2) We have to ask for a compensation of US $460 to cover the loss incurred.

3) The consignment covering our Order No. 5792 arrived last week. We are sorry to find that there is a shortage of 1,605 kilos, though the packing remains intact. It is beyond doubt that the shortage occurred prior to shipment. Therefore, we must lodge against you a claim for US $1,500. In support of our claim, we are sending you a survey report issued by C.C.I.B.

☞ **C. Read the following letter and learn how to name specific actions to remedy the problem.**

Dear Mr Xia,

　　We would refer to your consignment of leathers (Order No. 120 – 05) which arrived this morning.

　　On opening the cases, we found that we have received the wrong goods, the shipment being apparently intended for another buyer.

　　Please advise us when we can expect to receive our order, as some of our customers have been waiting for up to six weeks.

　　Please also let us know what we are to do with the leathers now in our possession.

Yours truly,
Fu Changrong

Translate the following sentences into English.

1) 请立即对此事进行调查,并通知我们迟延的原因。

2) 请于 6 月 20 日之前将替换品送来。

3) 您能今天就派人来修理吗?

☞ **D. Read the following letter and learn how to negotiate about adjustments.**

Dear Sirs,

　　We wish to refer to our letter of May 28 and your letters of April 10, 15, and 20, in which you made a claim on our last shipment of spare parts.

　　After further consultation with the manufacturers of the goods, we regret to say that we are unable to come to any positive result which would help clear the situation.

　　Our manufacturers think that by a few traces of rust no harm could be done to those spare parts. They are not precision instruments after all, which would need different packing. Our manufacturers therefore conclude that there is no valid ground for complaint so long as such a defect does not in the least affect the use of the goods.

　　In consequence, we consider it difficult to file a claim against the manufacturers. Nevertheless, we are prepared to straighten out the matter in an amicable way by paying you a rebate of 5% so as to start with a clean slate.

　　We hope that you will accept our proposal for settlement of the pending case so that we may continue doing business with you shortly.

　　We look forward to your early reply.

Yours sincerely,
[Signature]

Fill in the blanks with the proper forms of the words given in the brackets.

1) We are prepared to make you a reasonable _____ (compensate) but not the amount you _____ (claim), because we cannot see why the _____ (lose)

should be 50% more than the actual value of the goods. Please reconsider the matter.

2) It would not be fair if the _____ (lose) be totally imposed on us, as the liability rests with both parties. We are ready to pay 50% of the _____ (lose) only.

3) The wrong pieces may be _____ (return) per next available steamer for our account, but it is preferable if you can dispose of them in your market.

4) We may compromise, but the _____ (compensate) should, in no case, exceed Stg. 257. Otherwise, this case will be submitted to _____ (arbitrate).

11.3 Writers' Workshop: Create an Appropriate Tone

Tone may be defined as the overall impression or feeling a message conveys to its reader. In writing business messages you should match tone to purpose. Try to strike a balance between being formal and being familiar. Be confident, but not aggressive. Be courteous but not stuffy. Try to sound natural without becoming too chummy. Try to create a friendly and sincere tone so that your readers will understand that you sincerely wish to be of service. Your purpose in writing is to persuade them to agree with you. Therefore, adopt a tone that will allow you to be convincing. Remember what is said is often not as significant as how it is said. Compare the different wording and tone employed when turning down an offer:

 a. Unfortunately, we got a better offer. (Poor tone)
 b. We were pleased to receive your offer, but ... (Better tone)

Positive Tone vs Negative Tone

Words with negative meaning ought to be avoided in writing to make claims or complaints, for they usually hurt the reader's feelings or make an impression on him that he is reproached. Furthermore, such words and expressions as "claim", "complaint", "criticism", "fail", "defective", "mistake", "neglect", "ignore", "carelessness", and "You can't ... " are usually of negative meaning and most probably cause you trouble as well as unpleasant feelings to the reader.

Therefore, you should use such words and expressions with positive meaning as "You may ... ", "We'll ... ", "You will be happy that ... " to tell the reader what he can do instead of what he can't do. Please read and compare the following pairs of sentences.

 ※ You failed to include your credit card number, so we can't mail your order.
 Cf. We'll mail your order as soon as we receive your credit card number.
 ※ You can't park in Lot H until May 1.
 Cf. You may park in Lot H starting May 1.

"You-attitude" vs "We-attitude"

In BE communications, you need to put yourself in the reader's shoes, that is, to take "You-attitude". "You-attitude" does not simply mean being polite with a lot of "Thank you", but it also means that you show your consideration and care of the reader because you are making a request upon the addressee. Just see the use of "You" in the following examples:

- *Please enclose the sales receipt with the merchandise, so that we can process your refund promptly.*
- *University Books will open a new store here to serve you.*

11.3.1 Group work

Work in a group of 3 or 4 to discuss the following sentences and detecting the problem with them. Then make improvement on the sentences.

a) You won't be sorry that ...

b) The problem cannot be solved without the aid of top management.

c) You must pay your bill by the tenth of each month to receive a discount of 2 percent.

d) If my qualifications meet your requirements ...

e) We trust this is a satisfactory arrangement ...

f) In the event that we cannot meet the deadline, we will refund your money.

g) Unfortunately, we got a better offer.

11.3.2 Rewriting the following sentences by adopting "You-attitude"

1) If our above desire coincides with yours, we'd like to have your specific enquiries so that we can send our illustrated catalogue and price list for your reference without delay.

2) We must receive your receipt with the merchandise before we can process your refund.

3) We request you to introduce us to some of the most reliable importers of the same lines.

4) You are requested to send us all the necessary information regarding your products for export, with details of your prices and terms of payment.

5) University Books is proud to open a new store here.

11.3.3 Comment and improvement

Make your comment and improvement on the following letter.

Dear Mr Watt,

This is to apply for a position in labor relations with your company.

At present, I am studying in labor at Nanjing University and will graduate with a bachelor degree of business administration. I major in labor relations. I have taken all the courses, such as computer, law, and economics.

I have had good working experience as a clerk, truck driver, and repairer. You can see details on the enclosed résumé. I am confident that I am well qualified for your position and I like to work for a company of your size and description.

I must make a quick decision on my career, so I request that you write me soon. I will be available for an interview on May 20 and 21.

Sincerely yours,

[Signature]

Unit 12　Agency

Learning Objectives

- ✓ *learning about agency*
- ✓ *learning how to negotiate about agency*
- ✓ *learning how to perform relative functions of language and communication*
- ✓ *learning how to write concisely*

Identify Problems in the Following Writing & Comment

Good morning,

　　May I take this opportunity to introduce myself to you, my name is "Andina", and I am a Booker and Negotiator in the Entertainment Industry, and we have the following artistes and attractions on our computer listing. Star Entertainment is in the process of reproducing a new brochure, and as you are already on our mailing list, your copy of our 2005 Edition will be automatically forwarded to you on its publication.

　　In the meantime should you require one of our artistes for a personal appearance, an opening, exhibition, after-dinner speaking, promotional or publicity purposes, or maybe you just have a general enquiry on prices and availability, but, whatever your requirements, please do not hesitate to contact me.

　　You will also find enclosed some of our Golden Coupons for your own use, but may I suggest one in your card file, one on your telephone, and give one to a friend. I look forward to hearing from you.

　　　　　　　　　　　　　　　　　　　　　　　　　　　　With best wishes

　　　　　　　　　　　　　　　　　　　　　　　　　　　　Andina

12.1　Experience & Practice

12.1.1　Learning about agency

☞ **A. Brief introduction**

Questions: Why is agency necessary in international trade? And what do you need to do before appointing an agent?

　　When a company wants to expand its business, it often turns to agents for help. It is more convenient and economical for a foreign trade company to do their buying and selling business through agencies abroad, because a foreign agent is well familiar with the market conditions in which he will operate, and he knows what goods and what prices are best suited to his area. So many transactions in international trade are handled not by direct negotiation between the Buyer and Seller but by agencies, usually in the country of the Buyer.

① General and Exclusive Agents

There are chiefly two types of agents: general agent and sole/exclusive agent.

A general agent may be a firm or a person who acts under instructions from his principal to sell or buy on the best terms obtainable. He charges a commission for his services under certain agreement or contract. Similar to a general agent, an exclusive agent, also called sole agent, may be a firm or a person who acts exclusively for his foreign principal to sell in a certain area on a commission basis certain commodities supplied by the principal under some agreement. The sole agent will not sell other goods that compete with the principal's, but there is no such undertaking for a general agency.

② What to Do Before Appointing an Agent

Prior to the appointment of an agent, the principal should make a careful investigation about the qualification, experience and integrity of the firm appointed, such as:

- The reliability and financial soundness of the prospective agent
- His marketing and sales promoting skills
- His market connections and sales channels
- Whether the prospective agent is also an agent of similar goods

③ Points to Remember

When you write to ask to be an agent, you ought to follow the plan below:

- Open with a statement about agency.
- Make a brief introduction to yourself, particularly to the advantages you have concerning the business in question.
- Expect a positive answer to the request for agency.

B. Experience by reading and answering questions.

a. Read the following letter and answer the questions.

- *What does the writer ask to do in the letter?*
- *How is the letter written? Concise?*

Dear Sirs,

We are glad to learn that you are looking for a reliable firm with good connections in the synthetic fabric trade to represent you in the US.

We have been in this line for more than fifteen years. We import synthetic fabric from China for our buyers. As we have had experiences in marketing products like yours and we are familiar with buyers' needs, we are confident that we could expand your sales in the US.

We look forward to the possibility of representing your products in here.

                  Yours sincerely,
                  [Signature]

b. Read the following letter and answer the questions.
- *Does the writer agree to grant the agency? What kind of agency is allowed?*
- *How is the letter written? Concise and to-the-point?*

Dear Sirs,

Thank you for your letter of January 24 and also your proposal for an agency agreement between us. Considering your excellent performance in pushing the sales of our manufactures and the satisfactory business records, we have decided to appoint you as our exclusive agent for our Panda Brand Televisions in the territory of Iraq.

We have drawn up a draft exclusive agency agreement in which the terms and conditions are stipulated in details. Please examine it and tell us if they meet with your approval.

We hope the establishment of agency will further expand the business to our mutual benefit.

Yours sincerely,
[Signature]

12.1.2 Practice

A. Read the following conversation and then on Miss White's behalf, write a reply on its basis.

Mr Lin: Miss White, I think you've already received our letter which I expressed our desire to be an agent for your products.

Miss White: Yes. Mr Lin, that's a week ago.

Mr Lin: What's your opinion?

Miss White: Er ... To be frank, Mr Lin, after I've read your letter, I feel that it's not a mature time for you to act as a sole agent for our products.

Mr Lin: Why not?

Miss White: Here are several points to support my idea. First of all, you are not quite experienced in trading with this kind of products. You'll need some time to find out the potential market ability. Second, the annual order and turnover you promised is much lower than we expected.

Mr Lin: But this figure is only our first year's aim. We'll gradually enlarge our selling amount later. Though the order is not big, it will help you to establish your market channel and expand the influence of your products in this country, don't you think so?

Miss White: This is not wrong. However, it's not the only way to push sales. We may make full use of our advertisements and sales force to enlarge our sales market.

Mr Lin: But these will cost more and the effect may not be as evident as to have an agent.

Miss White: I understand your meaning, Mr Lin. Thank you for your good intentions. We'll consider your request when the chance serves.

☞ **B. Complete the following letter according to the Chinese given in the brackets and then write a reply to it according to the requirements.**

- Express your thanks and pleasure to the recipient for his invitation to be an agent.
- Tell that you have enclosed a short account of your activities together with the names of three companies with whom you have had dealings for a number of years.
- Express your expectation of receiving agency agreement.

Dear Sirs,

　　We ＿＿＿＿＿＿＿＿＿＿①＿＿＿＿＿＿＿＿＿＿（很想扩大出口）to Africa of top-class office furniture, and are looking for ＿＿＿＿＿＿＿＿＿＿②＿＿＿＿＿＿＿＿＿＿（代表我方的合适代理）.

　　If you are interested for the Kenya agency for a twelve-month ＿＿＿③＿＿＿（试用期）, we should be pleased to send you the draft agreement stating ＿＿＿＿④＿＿＿＿（代理条款）. We enclose for your information a copy of our latest catalogue and price list.

　　We look forward to hearing from you and to receiving your reference.

　　　　　　　　　　　　　　　　　　　　　　　Yours sincerely,
　　　　　　　　　　　　　　　　　　　　　　　[Signature]

12.1.3　Case study & practice

　　Now you are a saleman in Shanghai Seagull Camera Co., Ltd. and you are trying to find agents for "Seagull" cameras in Africa. Here is a sample letter you may imitate when you compose a letter by employing the following information given in Chinese.

1) 告知经中国银行上海分行介绍,致信中国银行开普敦分行的科长(Corporate Section Manager)询问有关开普敦产品代理事宜。
2) 自我简介一下,并讲明出口南非的意图。
3) 请对方将此函转交开普敦有意代理的公司,并说明随函附寄产品目录和价目表。

Sample Letter

Dear Corporate Section Manager,

　　We are writing to enquire about agents for our products in Bahrain. Your branch in Orlando, Florida, has told us that you may be able to help us.

　　We manufacture radio telephones. At present, we export to Europe and Latin America, but we would like to start exporting to the Arabian Gulf.

　　Could you please forward this letter to any companies in Bahrain that might be interested in representing us? We enclose some of our catalogues.

　　　　　　　　　　　　　　　　　　　　　　　Sincerely yours,
　　　　　　　　　　　　　　　　　　　　　　　[Signature]

12.2 Communicating & Writing Skills

☞ **A. Read the following letters and learn to propose to be an agent and make a reply.**

⊕ **A letter asking to be an agent**

Dear Sirs,

The demand for toiletries in the United Arab Emirates has shown a marked increase in recent years. We are sure that there is a considerable market here for your products.

Every sign shows that an advertising campaign, even on a modest scale, would produce very good results if it were backed by an efficient system of distribution.

We are well-known distributors of over 15 years' standing, with branches in most of the principal towns. With knowledge of the local conditions, we feel we have the experience and the resources necessary to bring about a market development of your trade in this country. Reference to the Embassy of the United Arab Emirates and to Middle East Services and Sales Limited would enable you to verify our statement.

If you were to appoint us as your agents, we should be prepared to discuss the rate of commission. However, as the early work on development would be heavy, we feel that 10 percent on orders placed during the first 12 months would be a reasonable figure. As the market would be new to you and customers largely unknown, we would be quite willing to act on a del credere basis in return for an extra commission of 2.5 percent to cover the additional risk.

We hope you will see a worthwhile opportunity in our proposal, and that we may look forward to your early decision.

Yours sincerely,
[Signature]

⊕ **Reply to the above letter**

Dear Sirs,

We are interested in your proposals of July 8 but, though favorably impressed by your views, are concerned that even a modest advertising campaign may not be worthwhile. We therefore suggest that we first test the market by sending you a representative selection of our products for sale on our account.

In the absence of advertising we realize that you would not have an easy task, but the experience gained would provide a valuable guide to future prospects. If the arrangement was successful we would consider your suggestion for a continuing agency.

Meanwhile, if you are willing to receive a trial consignment, we will allow commission at 12.5 percent, with an additional 2.5 percent del credere commission, commission and expenses to be sent against your monthly payments.

Please let us know as soon as possible if this arrangement is satisfactory to you.

Yours faithfully,
[Signature]

Complete the following sentences by translating the Chinese in the brackets.

1) We take the liberty of addressing this letter to you _____ _____（询问你们是否愿意任命我们作你们的代理,把你们的羊毛产品的出口扩大到我国）for the sale of your products.

2) We'd like to _____（签订一项独家代理协议）with you on our electric fans for a period of two years. We appoint you as our sole agent according to the terms mentioned in your letter of September 13, 2002.

3) In view of our experience and extensive business connections, we hope you will appoint us your _____（本区域的独家代理）.

4) We are _____（给你们写信是关于独家代理的事宜）.

5) We hope to come to an arrangement with you _____（就代理的事宜）.

B. Read the following letters and learn how to write a letter looking for a sole agent and a reply.

⊕ **A letter looking for a sole agent**

Dear Sirs,

Because of the steady rise in demand for our Automatic Washing Machines in your country, we have decided to appoint an agent to handle our export trade in your areas. When we last met at the Guangzhou Fair, you mentioned that you might be interested in an agency and we can perhaps come to some arrangement.

There are signs of a promising market for our products and a really active agent could no doubt bring about a big increase in our sales. Aware of your wide experience in this trade and of your connections with the principal buyers in your country, we feel that your firm is the right one to do this and have pleasure in offering you a sole agency.

Should you not be able to accept it, perhaps you could recommend some other reliable and well-established firm, with whom we might approach. We hope, however, that you yourself will accept. If you decide to do so, please state the terms on which you would be willing to represent us.

Yours sincerely,

[Signature]

⊕ **Reply to an offer of agency**

Dear Sirs,

Thank you for your letter of June 25 and for your invitation to represent you in our market. It is true that there has recently been a growing demand here for your products, but we doubt whether your expectation of future demand will be fulfilled. We hope you are right, but at the same time feel bound to mention competition from other manufacturers will probably be increased if the demand continues to grow. Even so, we are quite willing to accept the agency for a trial period provided you are prepared to support our efforts with reasonable publicity, as by advertising during the first six months or so.

We shall welcome your further comments on the suspicion and request made in the above.

Yours sincerely,

[Signature]

Write something in the following situations.

1) You are planning to expand your business to the USA and ask if your counterpart in the USA is interested in representing you as your sole agent.
2) Reply that you have already appointed sole agents in the addressee's territory.
3) Tell the applicant to double their efforts to build up a large turnover so as to qualify for sole agent appointment.
4) Tell that the minimum yearly turnover of US $50,000 is the condition for entrusting the addressee with exclusive agency.
5) Tell the applicant that the time is not ripe for the discussion of the question of exclusive agency.

C. Read the following letter and learn how to negotiate about the terms for agency.

Dear Sirs,

<u>Re: Agency Agreement</u>

We are pleased to learn that you have offered to act as our sole agent for marketing our footwear in the US. After a careful review of our business relations and your past efforts in pushing the sales of our products, we have decided to entrust you with the exclusive agency for our footwear in your country. We set out below the main terms to be covered in the Agency Agreement and should like you to confirm them before drafting the formal agreement.

- The agency to be a sole agency for marketing our footwear in the US.
- No sales of competing products to be made in the US either on your account or on account of any other firms.
- All customers' orders to be transmitted to us immediately for prompt supply.
- All goods supplied to be invoiced by us direct to customers, with copies to you.
- A commission of 5% based on FOB values of all goods shipped to the US, whether on order placed through you or not, payable at the end of each quarterly period.
- A special del credere commission of 2.5% to be added.
- Credit terms not to be given or promised to any customer without our express consent.
- Customers to settle their accounts with us direct, and we to send you a statement at the end of each month of all payments received by us.
- The agency to operate as from January 1 next year for a period of one year, automatically renewable on expiration for a similar period unless notice is given to the contrary.
- All questions or differences arising under our agreement to be solved through consultation or to be referred to arbitration if necessary.

Would you please confirm these terms? We will then arrange for formal agreement to be drafted and copies sent for your signature.

Yours sincerely,
[Signature]

Match the parts marked 1)−5) with those marked a)−e).

1) We would like to know on what terms

2) Guarantee of minimum volume of business is a premise to
3) After careful consideration, we decided to
4) The new rate of commission is
5) As this business is done on principal-to-principal basis, we will not consider

a) paying any commission
b) to take effect from the next transaction
c) allow you 2% commission
d) the signing of the agency agreement
e) you would be willing to represent us

12.3　Writers' Workshop: Conciseness & Simplicity

Conciseness vs Wordiness

Business writing ought to be concise rather than wordy. Traditional BE letter writing was full of redundant and obsolete wording, which must be deleted or updated to meet the requirement for modern or contemporary BE writing. Please compare:

　※ There are many requirements we must meet.
　Cf. We must meet many requirements.
　※ In view of the fact that the workers are working in three shifts of eight hours, shipment can be made on time.
　Cf. Since the workers are working in three shifts of eight hours, shipment can be made on time.

As can be seen from the above examples, the requirement for modern or contemporary BE writing is to write in concise and direct style.

Simplicity vs Complexity

Long, complicated sentences may be confusing for readers while shorter and simpler sentences are clearer and easier to understand. Traditional BE letter writers tended to write long, complicated sentences which were difficult to understand. Now the tendency for modern BE writing is simplicity and clearness, which are realised by using short words and sentences.

12.3.1　Group work

Work in a group of three or four and try to make the following sentences more concise and more forceful.

a) It is our plan to open a new branch office in New Deli.
b) The plans for the new building will be carefully studied by Mr Allen, one of our architects.
c) David is of the conviction that service has improved.
d) This policy exists for the purpose of preventing dishonesty.

e) The salesman who was most successful received the best rewards.

f) We will deliver the goods in the near future.

12.3.2 Rewriting each of the following sentences into 2 or 3 ones

1) Working in an export company requires a lot of specialist knowledge, including a mastery of the complex documentation, an awareness of the various payment methods that are available and the ability to communicate with foreign customers in writing.

2) One of the most difficult aspects of corresponding with people you have not met face-to-face is establishing a personal relationship with them in order to show them that you are not just a letter-writing machine but a real person.

3) As requested, I enclose our new catalogue and feel sure that you will find within many items to interest you, particularly our new range of colours that will brighten up your office and keep your staff feeling happy.

12.3.3 Comment and improvement

Comment on the following letter and see what improvement you can make.

Gentlemen:

In regard to the first shipment against our Contract No. 1234, we wrote you on 7th instant that part of the goods was not in conformity with the contracted specifications. We requested you to give us explanations and advise us how you would deal with the matter, but up to now we have not yet received any reply.

So we regret to say that we can not accept the second lot of goods. We requested you to postpone shipment of this shipment for the time being. It goes without saying that we have no obligations whatever in this matter.

We are looking forward to your reply.

                    Yours faithfully,
                    [Signature]

Unit 13　Social Letters

Learning Objectives
- ✓ learning about social letter writing
- ✓ learning how to write social letters
- ✓ learning how to perform relative functions of language and communication
- ✓ learning how to be complete in writing

Identify Problems in the Following Writing & Comment

Dear Cat,

　　I've accepted a new position that is a good career move in terms of money and responsibilities. As you know, you told me a promotion and a raise aren't in my future here this year. I really enjoy working at Inclusive Insurance but need to move on. I'll be glad to train my replacement in the remaining time. My last day here will be July 3.

Best wishes,
Don

13.1　Experience & Practice

13.1.1　Learning about social letter writing

☞ **A. Brief introduction**

Questions: *Can you list any commonly-used social letters? How do you usually write these social letters?*

① Main Types of Social Letters

　　In international trade, some letters do not discuss business affairs directly, but they are necessary in maintaining a good business relationship. These letters written to build and promote a positive relationship between communicators are generally called social letters, or goodwill letters. There are many types of social letters, of which the four types most commonly-used in business life are letters of invitation, letters of introduction, letters of congratulation, letters of comfort, resignation letters, apology letters and thank-you letters.

② How to Write Social Letters

Most of the social letters express personal feelings, but they should follow the layout and the style of a business letter. A social letter should be brief, clear and sincere. The aim of the letter should be clearly stated at the beginning of a letter so that the recipient can be informed efficiently at first glance. It should also be sincere in tone. An improper tone may arouse suspicion on the motivation of the writer and even a feeling of antipathy. Besides, these letters should be written without delay. They are easier to write when the situation is fresh in our mind. A prompt response to the event also means more to the recipient, for example, a prompt thank-you letter carries the hidden message that you care and that you consider the event to be important.

A successful social letter should also be selfless, specific, sincere and short. Being selfless means to be sure to focus the message solely on the receiver, not the sender. Being specific means to personalize the message by mentioning specific incidents or characteristics of the receiver. Being sincere means to let your words express your genuine feelings. Being short means to avoid wordiness.

③ Points to Remember when Writing Invitation Letters

Invitations are written in the deductive pattern and are relatively short. When you write invitation letters, you ought to follow the steps below:

- Invite the reader to a certain event.
- Offer a reason for the gathering.
- Give the date, time, and place of the gathering.

④ Points to Remember when Writing Thank-you Letters

A thank-you letter covering a business situation must be sent promptly. It must also sound sincere. When you write thank-you letters, you ought to follow the steps below:

- Begin with a statement of thanks.
- Be specific about what is appreciated, which reflects a sincere feeling of gratitude.
- End with a positive and genuine statement.

⑤ Points to Remember when Writing Apology Letters

Apologies are necessary for your own peace of mind and for the good relationship with the offended person. When you have to apologize, you must be sincere, direct and brief.

The writer should apologize directly and use general terms to avoid reinforcing the unpleasantness of the errors. That reinforcement would work against the purpose of apology. When you write apology letters, you ought to follow the following steps:

- Begin with an apology and reveal the purpose of the letter.
- Present the specific situation for which you apologize. And discuss methods to redress the situation, if needed.
- Close with a positive look to future business or personal relationship.

⑥ Points to Remember when Writing Letters of Comfort

A comfort letter is a kind of letter in which the writer expresses his comfort about the misfortune which happens to an individual or an organization, or the writer just gives his greetings to an individual or a company about some achievements. In business, comfort letters are very helpful in maintaining good relationship between business partners.

When you write comfort letters, you ought to follow the following steps:
- Start with a statement of sympathy.
- Follow with sentences about mutual experiences or relationship.
- Close with some expressions of comfort and affection.

B. Experience by reading and answering questions.

a. Read the following letter and answer the questions.
- *What kind of letter is the following one?*
- *What does the writer ask the addressee to do in the closing of the letter?*

Dear Mr Smith,

We would like to extend to you an invitation for your visit to the 10th Chinese Export Commodities Fair in Guangzhou, which is to be held from September 6 to September 16. All of our new items will be on display in the Fair. Our manager and sales representatives will be there to meet you and conduct negotiations with you. We sincerely hope you could come for a visit in the Fair. We are confident that our meeting at the Fair will be fruitful and lead to the advance of our business relations.

Please confirm your visit at your earliest convenience so that we could make the necessary arrangements.

Sincerely yours,
Wan Yuan

---

b. Read the following letter and answer the questions.
- *What kind of letter is the following one? Does the writer confirm his visit?*
- *What does the writer do in the second paragraph?*

Dear Mr Wan,

Thank you for inviting me to the 10th Chinese Export Commodities Fair in Guangzhou and I accept it with great pleasure.

As a regular customer of your company, I always find your products innovative in design and superior in quality. I am very interested in the new items that are to be displayed at the Fair.

Sincerely yours,
Paul Smith

C. Read and comment on the following letters.

a. Letter of Introduction

Dear Mr Brown,

　　I take pleasure in introducing the bearer of this letter, Mr Tang Huimin, a great friend of mine, who wants to secure a position in New York. Mr Tang has been a manager in Pearl Hotel in Guangzhou since last year. He is a wonderful man to know and I am sure he will be delighted and charmed to meet you. He can speak English very well, but as he is an entire stranger in your locality, he should appreciate any assistance you may be able to give him.

　　With best wishes for your kind consideration and attention.

Yours sincerely,

John Lin

b. Letter of Congratulation

Dear Bob,

　　Congratulations on your promotion to become the vice president of the company!

　　If you feel like holding a celebration, will you let me take you to dinner and the movies, as a sort of promotion treat? You name the day. And in the meantime, I wish you success in the new position!

Cordially,

Tom Hilton

c. Thank-you Letter

Dear Joe,

　　I very much appreciate your having shown me around your plant last week. It was quite an experience and I was very much impressed by your advanced system in the computer room. The many pamphlets you gave me on the equipment will be very useful to our company. Thank you very much again for your kindness. I hope you will give me an opportunity to reciprocate your kindness.

Best wishes,

Mary

d. Apology Letter

Dear Mr Zhang,

　　I am sorry for not being able to send you immediately our catalog and price list you asked for in your letter dated May 5.

　　We appreciate your interest in our products, but the present catalog does not include some new items we have recently developed. Besides, the increasingly rising cost in labor has pushed the cost of our products higher; therefore, our prices will have to be adjusted accordingly. Now we are in the process of making new catalog and price list to portrait all these changes. We will send them to you after they are ready in 10 days. Meanwhile, we would be glad to offer information that you need for particular products. Just send your request by e-mail.

We are looking forward to the opportunity of providing our products to you.

Yours sincerely,
Adam Evens

e. Letter of Comfort

Dear Mrs Corbin,

I was so sorry to learn of your illness. You must hurry and get well! Everybody in the company misses you, and we're all hoping you'll be back soon.

Mr. Burke joins me in sending best wishes for your speedy recovery.

Sincerely yours,
Mary Burke

f. Letter of Introduction

Dear Tom,

I'm writing to introduce you to Janice Dolan, who I have the pleasure of being acquainted with through the Brandon Theater Group. I am the Technical Director for the group, as you know, and I have worked with Janice on several local theater projects. She is a terrific stage manager with over ten years of experience.

Janice is interested in relocating to the San Francisco area in the near future and would appreciate any recommendations you could offer her for conducting a job search for a theater position and any help you can provide with the logistics of relocating to California.

I have attached her CV for your review and you can contact her at jdolan@ email. com or 555-555-5555. Thank you in advance for any assistance you can provide.

Sincerely,
Barbara Smith

13.1.2 Practice

A. On Mr Emerson's behalf, write a letter to thank Wu Yan according to the following dialogue.

Mr Emerson: Mr Wu, thanks a lot for your help and hospitality to me.

Wu Yan: You're welcome, Mr Emerson. And here's a present for you from our corporation.

Mr Emerson: Oh, thank you! It's very kind of you. Ah, it's a porcelain.

Wu Yan: I hope you like the design.

Mr Emerson: Yes, it's lovely! I've been wanting something like this for a long time. Thanks ever so much.

Wu Yan: I'm glad you like it.

☞ **B. Read the following letter of introduction and rearrange the paragraphs into the right order.**

Dear Bob,
　① Chuck is district manager of Forster & Company, and in fact, does the same type of work that you are doing for your company. I feel sure each of you will enjoy knowing the other.
　② Needless to say, I shall appreciate any courtesy you may extend to Chuck during his brief stop in Hong Kong.
　③ My good friend and former colleague, Chuck Conwell, will present this note to you when he stops in Hong Kong on his way to the East Asia.
　　　　　　　　　　　　　　　　　　　　　　　　Sincerely yours,
　　　　　　　　　　　　　　　　　　　　　　　　Jack Kennedy

13.1.3　Case study & practice

☞ **A. Read the following letter of invitation to a sales conference and write a reply to decline it.**

Dear Mr Godwin,
　On behalf of Yonglin Inc., it is my great pleasure to invite you to our annual sales conference, which will be held on September 25 – 30, 2021 at the Heping International Conference Centre in Hangzhou. Enclosed you will find the schedule for the conference and the accommodation arrangements.
　We would appreciate it if you could confirm your presence at your earliest convenience. Please contact me at 0571 – 80958675.
　　　　　　　　　　　　　　　　　　　　　　　　Yours sincerely,
　　　　　　　　　　　　　　　　　　　　　　　　Zhang Yun

☞ **B. As a business associate, write a letter of congratulation to Mr Norton on his advancement to the presidency of his company.**

13.2　Communicating & Writing Skills

☞ **A. Read the following letter and learn how to make an invitation.**

Dear Mr Black,
　To celebrate the 10th anniversary of Shenzhen Trading Co., Ltd, we are holding a dinner party at Hilton Hotel in Shenzhen from 7:00 p.m. to 9:30 p.m. on Saturday, June 6.
　You are cordially welcome to the party so that we can express our sincere appreciation for your generous support. For your information, the party will be attended by other business elites such as Mr

Zang Hong and Li Peng. We believe that this may offer many of us an excellent opportunity to get acquainted with each other.

We do hope that you will be able to join us on this occasion, and look forward to meeting you at the party.

Sincerely yours,
Yang Ming

Write a letter in the following situations by using the expressions given below.

We are writing to invite you	We would like to invite you
It would be a great pleasure to	We are honoured to invite you
I take great pleasure in inviting you to	Will you come to
Our company cordially invite you to	

1) Your company will be commencing production on April 16. Invite your business partner and his wife to come to the celebration.
2) There will be a reception in honour of the Chinese trade delegation. Invite Mr Liu to be present at the reception.
3) Invite one of your friends to come and celebrate the opening of your store in the Shopping Centre.
4) Express your hope that your friend can join you for the opening ceremony of your branch office.

B. Read the following letter and learn how to make introductions.

Dear Mr Kwok,

This letter will introduce Professor Chen of Zhejiang Normal University of Finance & Economics, a good friend of mine, who is at present interested in obtaining data on Communication Studies. Therefore, I would very much appreciate it if you could kindly give him any relevant data from your Research Institute.

Sincerely yours,
Fay Show

Study the following examples.
1) This is to introduce ...
2) I should like to introduce ...
3) This letter will introduce ...
4) It is my pleasure to write a letter of introduction ...

☞ **C. Read the following letter and learn to extend congratulations.**

Dear Mr Kara,
    I have learned with great delight that you are establishing your own advertising company and starting business today. I'd like to add my voice to the chorus of congratulation from all sides. Due to your brilliant background and rich experience, you will greatly succeed in the near future.
    If there is anything in which I can be of assistance, please let me know. I wish you success of your company and look forward to close cooperation with you in the development of business.
Yours sincerely,
Carter Boswell

Complete the following sentences with the words or expressions given below.

> achieving   congratulate   It was encouraging to   congratulations

1) _____ on your promotion to become CEO of the company.
2) Please accept our heartiest congratulations on your _____ initial sales of 30,000 tons.
3) _____ you on your being promoted to the position of Senior Sales Manager.
4) _____ learn that you managed to be in the No. 1 position in sales in your market for fiscal 2008.

☞ **D. Read the following letter and learn how to express thanks.**

Dear Sirs,
    We have confirmed by fax accepting your firm order of 15th May. As this is your first order with us, we must write to tell you how glad we were to receive it and to thank you for the opportunity you have given us to supply the goods you need.
    We hope our handling of this order will lead to further business between us and to a happy and lasting cooperation.
Yours sincerely,
[Signature]

Study the following examples.
1) Thank you for ...
2) We should like to express my sincere thanks for ...
3) I would like to express my appreciation for ...
4) It was most kind of you to give me ...
5) I am grateful to you for ...

E. Read the following letter and learn to express apologies.

Dear Mr White,

    In order not to have any misunderstanding between us, please accept my apology for the manner in which our security officer spoke to you this morning.

    Our security officers had been instructed to keep certain parking spaces open for company officers, but they should have remembered their obligation to be courteous and helpful. The chief of security has already disciplined the officer, asking him to attend the human relations seminars.

    When you call at our office again, you can expect efficiency and courtesy, which have been our goals for the past 12 years.

Sincerely yours,
Tom Brown

Translate the following sentences into English.

1）造成诸多不便,在此致歉。

2）我就装运合同与实际装运不符一事向您道歉。

3）对此次延误,谨表歉意。如果有任何其他问题,请立刻与我联络。

4）十分抱歉,我们不能及时寄送您7月30日信函所要的目录和价格表。

F. Read the following letter and learn to express comfort.

Dear Sam,

    The news of your accident just reached me this morning. I'm greatly shocked to learn that you were knocked down by a car yesterday. How are you feeling today?

    The only good thing about it is that your MD told me that you are progressing nicely. I hope that you are doing well after the operation, and that you'll be out of the hospital in about a week. I'm coming to see you on Sunday and trust that your condition will remarkably improve by then.

    A little package from Rose and me will reach you in a day or two. We hope the small thing will interest you.

    With every good wishes for your swift recovery!

Sincerely yours,
Li Ming

Study the following examples.

1) I just can't tell you how sorry I am to learn of sth. / to hear that ...

2) I'm greatly shocked to learn that ...

3) I send my love and deepest sympathy to both of you.

4) I'm sure you will have all your old health and strength back again.

5) How delighted I am to hear about your fine progress.

6) Please accept my most sincere sympathy and best wishes.

7) I'm really happy to hear that you'll be out of hospital soon and back in your company.

8) Best wishes for your speedy recovery.

9) It's wonderful news that all that's over now.

13.3 Writers' Workshop: Completeness vs Incompleteness

Completeness vs Incompleteness

In BE writing, message must be complete. Completeness refers to providing enough information so that the intention of the message is understood by the reader. A piece of business writing is successful and functions well only when it contains all the necessary information.

If writing is incomplete, it may cause unnecessary inconvenience and delay. In addition, incompleteness is not only impolite, but also leads to the recipients' unfavorable impression towards your firm. He may give up the deal if other firms can provide him with all the necessary information, or if he would not take the trouble of enquiring once again.

As you work hard for completeness, keep the following questions in mind:
- Why do you write?
- What are the facts supporting the reasons?
- Have you answered the questions asked or not?
- What is the reader expected to do?

13.3.1 Group work

Discuss in groups and revising the following sentences making them complete.

1) All sales representatives will meet at 9:00 on Monday.

2) Our Sales Manager will contact you soon.

3) My flight arrives at 6:30 on Wednesday.

13.3.2 Reading and completing the following letter of invitation to make it definite

Dear Mrs Jennings,

    Will you and Mr Jennings have dinner with us _____①_____ on Tuesday, _____②_____, at seven o'clock? It's a long time since we have had the pleasure of seeing you, and we do hope you can come.

                              Sincerely yours,

                              Elizabeth K. Benton

13.3.3 Comment and improvement

⊕ **Comment on the following letter and see what improvement you can make.**

Gentlemen,

                              Re: Computers

    With reference to your letter, we are pleased to accept your offer of ICM-4 computers as per your Quotation Sheet No. 9/04/2008.

    Please go ahead and apply for your Export License.

    As soon as we are informed of the number of your Export License, we will open the L/C by fax.

                                Yours truly,

                                [Signature]

Part Two

Internal Communication & BE Writing

Unit 14　Memorandums

learning Objectives

- ✓ learning about memo writing
- ✓ learning how to write memos
- ✓ learning how to perform relative functions of language and communication
- ✓ learning how to follow the trend for contemporary BE letter writing

---

Identify Problems in the Following Writing & Comment

To: Office Administrator
　From: Manager
　Subject: New Employee

　A new employee, John Anderson, will join us on 12 August and he will take charge of the marketing section. I should be obliged to you if you could arrange his desk in the room of marketing section.

14.1　Experience & Practice

14.1.1　Learning about memo writing

☞ **A. Brief introduction**

Questions: What is a memo? What functions and types of memos do you know?

① Definition of Memo & Difference between Memo and Letter

Memorandums or memos are business messages, which transmit information between colleagues or departments within a business organisation. As they go between co-workers and colleagues, they play an important part in keeping the different parts of a company in touch. Memos are simple because they do not have the formality of the letterhead, inside name and address, etc. And they are efficient because they convey the writers' ideas quickly and directly to the readers.

Memos, as a common means of internal communication, differ greatly from letters which usually go outside the company. Memos are generally less formal in style and tone than letters. Of course, memos can be formal in case the messages are highly serious, or they are sent, for example, to the president or the MD. Besides, memos are short, usually 2 pages at most. Longer messages are handled, instead, in the form of a report.

② Parts of a Memo

The format for memos varies from company to company. However, all memos, regardless of format, include the following five guide words:

- ♦ Memorandum or Memo, or Interoffice Memorandum
- ♦ Date: (the date on which the memo is written and sent)
- ♦ To: (the name of the person who will receive the message; the receiver's job title)
- ♦ From: (the name of the writer of the message)
- ♦ Subject/ Re: (the topic of the memo)

Some companies purchase or print their own memorandum stationary with the five guide words mentioned above. This saves the writer some time when preparing memos.

③ Functions and Types of Memos

Memos usually serve the following purposes:

➢ Give instructions or notify events which occurred;
➢ Seek information;
➢ Offer ideas and suggestions.

According to the above functions performed by memos, memos can be classified into:

- Announcement memos
- Instruction/directive memos
- Request memos
- Proposal memos
- Report memos
- Transmittal memos

④ Points to Remember

- Being brief

As a tool of efficient internal communication, memos should be concise. You can only convey what you intend to say. You should avoid redundancy in your message.

- Having a single topic.

An effective memo usually discuses a single topic; thus the reader may concentrate on the subject.

☞ **B. Experience by reading and answering questions.**

a. Read the following memo and answer the questions.

- *What kind of memo is the following one?*
- *How do you like the language used in the memo?*

MEMO

To: Paul Gray, Production Manager
From: Mary Zhang, Managing Director
Date: December 1, 2020
Subject: Making your suggestions on next year's production

　　The year of 2021 is one month away and it's time to plan for next year's production. Please have a think and make your suggestions on next year's production. Thanks!

b. Read the following memo and answer the questions.
- *What kind of memo is the following one?*
- *What kind of language is employed in the memo? Why?*

MEMO

To: Mary Zhang, Managing Director
From: Paul Gray, Production Manager
Date: 16 December 2021
Subject: Suggestions

　　Having checked our production capacity for the next year, I can suggest the following: Increase production by 20,000 bottles over a three-month period, while maintaining present production level of other lines.

　　Discontinue production of weaker line(s) and use the shortfall capacity for mineral water.

　　I hope one of these suggestions is suitable.

14.1.2　Practice

A. Read the following conversation and on Wang Gang's behalf, write a memo on its basis rearranging the meeting date.

Mr Wang:　　I'm so sorry to call you on such short notice but something's come up.
Mr Smith:　　You mean for this afternoon's meeting?
Mr Wang:　　That's right. I'm afraid I have to postpone it. Mr Scott got sick and I have to attend the Speechmaker's Symposium in his place. I'm leaving today, and I won't be back until a week from Friday.
Mr Smith:　　That's quite a while. Let's make it the week after you get back, then.
Mr Wang:　　That will be great. So it's two weeks from tomorrow, same time and place. I'm really sorry to do this to you.
Mr Smith:　　No problem at all. To tell you the truth, I could use the extra time in my schedule to catch up on some paperwork.

☞ **B. Read the following memos exchanged between Roberta Benetto and Jaques Duval and on Jaques Duval's behalf, write a reply.**

⊕ **Outgoing Memo**

To: Jaques Duval, Secretary
From: Roberta Benetto, Marketing
Date: May 21
Re: My visit to Beijing to attend Agents Workshop

　　Can you look through the flight details from Travel World and book a flight which arrives early in the morning of the 18th?
　　Thanks!

　　　　　　　　　　　　　　　　　　　　　　　　　　　　　　　　　　　　　RB

⊕ **Incoming Memo**

To: Roberta Benetto, Marketing
From: Jaques Duval, Secretary
Date: May 22
Re: Your flight to Beijing

　　I've checked the flight details from Travel World and found Flight AF 202 which arrives at 8:15 is the most suitable. How do you like it?

　　　　　　　　　　　　　　　　　　　　　　　　　　　　　　　　　　　　　JD

14.1.3　Case study & practice

☞ **A. Your boss has sent you the following memo. Complete it with the verbs in the box.**

| introduce | show | explain | arrange |

To: Paul Gething
From: Diana Skinner
Date: Friday, 28 November 2020

　　I have to go to Perth on Monday and Tuesday, but I'll be back on Wednesday. Henry Lee is arriving from the Hong Kong office on Monday evening. Could you:
　　　_____ the agenda of the training programme.
　　　_____ him around the company.
　　　_____ him to the Training Manager.
　　　_____ a meeting with the Production Manager.
　　Please apologize for me and tell him that I will see him at the factory on Wednesday morning. Thank you very much for your help.

　　　　　　　　　　　　　　　　　　　　　　　　　　　　　　　　　　　　　Diana

☞ **B. Read the following phone conversation and then write to Diana Skinner, reporting what you have done by sending an e-mail in the form of a memo.**

Paul: Paul Gething speaking.
Diana: Hello, Paul, this is Diana. How are things?
Paul: Oh hello, Diana. Fine, just fine. How's Perth?
Diana: OK, we've had a busy morning. I'm looking forward to getting home tomorrow! So, has Mr Lee arrived?
Paul: Oh yes, he arrived last night. I met him at the airport.
Diana: Oh good. And have you explained the programme to him?
Paul: Yes, I've explained it to him. We talked about it this morning before lunch. After lunch I showed him around the company.
Diana: Great, I'm glad you've shown him around. Now, has he met the Training Manager?
Paul: No, he hasn't. The Training Manager has been in a meeting all day.
Diana: Too bad. What about the meeting with the Production Manager? Have you arranged that yet?
Paul: I'm afraid not. She's been away from the office, but I've left a message for her.
Diana: Fine. Well, Paul, could you just send me an e-mail saying what you have and haven't done? Just in case I can't remember tomorrow!
Paul: Yes, I'll do it now.
Diana: Thanks. Goodbye.
Paul: Goodbye.

14.2 Communicating & Writing Skills

☞ **A. Read the following memo and learn how to request immediate feedback.**

MEMORANDUM
To: All members of staff, Northern Branch
From: K. L. J.
Date: 5 December 2020
Subject: Personal Computers

The board urgently requires feedback on our experience with PCs in Northern Branch. I need to know, for my report:

* What you personally use your PC for and your reasons for doing this. If you are doing work that was formerly done by other staff, please justify this.
* What software you use. Please name the programs.
* How many hours per day you spend actually using it.

---

* How your PC has not come up to your expectations.
* What unanticipated uses you have found for your PC, that others may want to share.

Please fax this information directly to me by 5 p.m. on Wednesday, 7 December. If you have any queries, please contact my assistant, Jane Simmonds, who will be visiting you on Tuesday, 6 December. Thank you for your help.

Write something in the following situations.

1) Tell the receiver that you need his/her feedback on the new computer systems.
2) You are planning to make some changes to the catalogue and price list. Ask the sales office for their opinion.
3) Ask the receiver to write a report before the next Board Meeting on June 1.
4) Tell the receiver to make a market research on the computers which are on sale in Hong Kong and the prices for them.
5) Ask the receiver to check the availability and the cost of tapes in these areas and provide you with a list by July 15.

B. Read the following memo and learn how to make instructions.

Memorandum

To: All Staff
From: Allen Smith, Administrative Officer
Date: May 12, 2020
Subject: Operating Instructions for New Copying Machines

A new photocopier has been installed in the general office. All staff is welcome to use it.

To ensure the copier's survival, it is important to keep the following procedures in mind.

◆ Use the machine for no longer than 30 minutes at a time.
◆ After use, allow the machine to cool for at least 5 minutes.
◆ Make sure the switch is turned off after use.

Please speak to me if you have any questions about the machine.

Complete the following sentences by using the verbs given in the box.

place	pay	serve	record

1) Please _____ attention to the problem.
2) _____ a note pad and a ball pen.
3) _____ the entire meeting session.
4) _____ a buffet dinner with dessert or soft beverages.

☞ **C. Read the following memos and learn how to make a notice.**

Memo 1

To: Sales Manager
From: General Manager
Date: Tuesday, March 11, 2021
Subject: Meeting on promotion expense
　　We're planning a meeting to discuss the promotion expense of our company. It's to be held on March 13, Thursday. at 15:00. You should take a detailed analysis report with you. Phone me if you have further questions.

Memo 2

From: Sales Supervisor
To: Area Sales Managers
　　We're gonna hold a sales meeting from 16:00 to 18:00 next Friday in Room 911. You're required to hand in analysis of the current market situation before the meeting. Please get them ready in advance.

Translate the following sentences into English.
1）请注意,明天(10 月 19 日,星期四)下午 4 点钟,网络停止运行 1 个或 2 个小时。
2）请注意,5 月 15 日星期一的会议改在 5 月 17 日星期三召开。
3）请注意,今年的圣诞派对将于 12 月 11 点至 15 点举行。

14.3　Writers' Workshop: Trend for Contemporary BE Letter Writing

　　Although BE letters still seem to be quite formal with the use of so many learned words and structures, business-letter writers have begun to write in a direct and concise way. American businesspeople consider that the spoken style used in business letters produces a more friendly atmosphere, so modern business letters tend to be something like a conversation by post or by e-mail.
　　As a result of the American influence, businesspeople have given up the stiff, formal and obsequious style of past generations in favor of the natural, conversational, unpretentious and inconspicuous modern style. The old-fashioned business language which made use of many hackneyed and stereotyped phrases has become obsolete.
Writing Short Words, Sentences and Paragraphs
　　Therefore, when we write business letters including faxes and memos, we ought to follow the following gold rules:

> - Use short sentences.
> - Put each separate idea in a separate paragraph. Number each of the paragraphs if it will help the reader to understand better.
> - Use short words that everyone can understand.
>
> In one word, we should keep it (our BE letter writing, especially memo writing) short and simple or sweet (KISS).

14.3.1 Group work

Work in groups of 3 or 4 to discuss the two different columns of words.

acknowledge	admit, think	advise	tell, say
anticipate	expect	application	use
endeavour	try	Esteemed Sir	Dear Sir
necessitate	require	substantial	large
utilize	use	variation	change

14.3.2 Reading the following conversation and comparing it with the memo on the same subject

⊕ **Conversation**

Mr W: Ah, Maria, I wanted to see you, um ... did I tell you that we're starting up the English classes again?

Maria: Oh, are you? Great, good. Where?

Mr W: Er ... in the training centre, hopefully. We're getting Roberts in again from ELS. So could you tell your people and let me have a list of names by, um, let's say Wednesday?

Maria: Yes, yes. Um, last time there was a bit of misunderstanding about the books they needed, um, about who was going to pay for them.

Mr W: Oh, really? Well, no problem this time, we'll provide the books. But they will have to do some homework outside work, make sure they realize that. Um ... or else there'll probably be some problems. Er ... there'll be two classes, by the way, an intermediate class and an advanced one. But there will be a limit in each of the classes of ... probably about twelve.

Maria: Oh, really, a limit of twelve? Ah, well, what if there are more people wanting to come? I mean, I can think of at least eight just in my department alone. Um ... how will we decide who can attend?

Mr W: Er ... mm, good point. Er ... I think we'll have to play that one by ear really.

Maria: OK, well, how about running another class?

Memo

From: HGW   To: Department managers
Date: 21/4/2021   Subject: In-service English classes

From Monday 8 May English classes will be held in the Training Centre (Room 317). There will be two groups: intermediate level (8:30 – 10:00) and advanced level (10:30 – 12:00). Please encourage your staff to attend one of the sessions. All teaching materials will be provided but students will be expected to do homework and preparation outside working hours.

Please send me the names of all interested staff by noon on Wednesday 26 April. They will be given an informal oral test during the first week in May so that we can decide which of the classes is best for them.

The size of each class will be limited to 12 participants.

                                                                HGW

14.3.3 Comment and improvement

Comment on the following memo before making any improvement.

Memo

Date: December 15
To: All Managers
From: Lois Lawrence
Re: Capping salary increases for employees

Commencing from January 1, we institute our new policy of capping salary increases at 3.5% for all employees. This is due to the fact that economy is turning down in our industry and we need to curtail our expenses in an endeavor to avoid further layoffs.

In order that you may prepare to answer any questions members of your department may have, a meeting is to be called, which you all must attend.

   Date: December 20
   Time: 10:30 to noon
   Place: Conference Room 200

We find it necessary to keep this in confidence until the announcement is to be made to everyone. That announcement will follow the meeting. If you have any queries, please give me a call.

Unit 15 Business Reports

Learning Objectives

- ✓ *learning about report writing*
- ✓ *learning how to write reports*
- ✓ *learning how to perform relative functions of language and communication*
- ✓ *learning how to write accurately and objectively*

Identify Problems in the Following Writing & Comment

Report on Staff Motivation

Introduction

I write this report to present the results of the recent survey of staff motivation. I base the findings on interviews with employees from all departments within the company.

Findings

A number of employees clearly suffer from a lack of motivation as a result of dissatisfaction in one of more areas of their work. I just outline the key findings below.

Staff feels undervalued by the company, both on a financial level and a personal level. They feel that the company's competitors offer higher levels of remuneration. The perception that managers are unappreciative of staff efforts is particularly noticeable in the Sales Department.

Certain employees fell under-challenged. The company is clearly not exploiting the potential of its human resources.

There appears to be a breakdown of communication in the Production Department. The confusion and resultant ill-feeling towards managers has the potential to disrupt production cycles.

Conclusion

We conclude that there are significant levels of dissatisfaction regarding certain issues within the company. Unless these issues are addressed as a matter of urgency, the consequent demotivation of staff will undoubtedly have a negative impact on the performance of the company.

Recommendations

We strongly recommend the following measures:
- An evaluation of job profiles needs to be made throughout the company to assess whether skills could be utilized more efficiently.
- A review of the current salary structure ought to involve comparison with similar organizations.

We find it essential to investigate and take action regarding communication in the Production and Sales Departments.

15.1　Experience & Practice

15.1.1　Learning about reports and communication in writing reports

☞ **A. Brief introduction**

Questions: *How many types of reports do you know? And how do you write reports effectively?*

① Definition & Classification of Reports

A report is an account of an event or events, or a subject giving information to a specific reader or group of readers, usually in response to a request or enquires for information.

Reports play a crucial role in business practice as most major or decisive actions are based on business reports. On the other hand, reports are also quite often used as a device to exchange information in and among businesses, for instance, reporting to upper management, giving instruction to the divisions, making proposals, presenting a result of an investigation, etc. If reports are well written, that is, data collected thoroughly, analysis done perceptively and comment made correctly, solution can be expected to draw in a wise way.

Report is a common way of communication in many different professions. Businesspeople write a wide range of reports under various names, such as business plan, business proposal, project report, financial plan, and performance report, etc.

Business reports can be classified according to their different content. There are routine reports, investigation reports, progress reports, and feasibility reports. A routine report is a report presented to upper management on the day-to-day work; an investigation report is the description of the findings of an investigation; a progress report provides information of an ongoing program; a feasibility report is an assessment of the practicality of a proposed plan or method. Other kinds of reports include incident reports, supervision reports, sales reports, improvement reports, market studies and research reports.

Business reports can be formal or informal according to the degree of formality. They can be short or long. They may be delivered orally or through e-mails, memos or letters, though formal business reports are customarily submitted in print.

② Three Parts of Formal Reports

Basically a formal report consists of three parts:

■ Prefatory parts
- Half-title page (It contains only the title of the report; it adds formality.)
- Title page (A report title page begins with the name of the report typed in upper case letters. Next comes "Presented to" and the name, title and organization of the individual receiving the report. Below it is "Prepared by" and the author's name

plus any necessary identification. The last item on the title page is the date of submission.)
- Transmittal letter or memo (The transmittal letter or memo typically announces the topic of the report and tells how it was authorized; briefly; describes the project; highlights the report's findings, conclusions and recommendations, if the reader is expected to be supportive; closes with appreciation for the assignment, instruction for the reader's follow-up actions.)
- Table of contents
- List of figures (For reports with some figures or illustrations, you may wish to include a list of figures to help the reader locate them.)
- Executive summary or abstract (It summarizes essential elements in a report. Whether you are writing an abstract or an executive summary, its length and complexity will be determined by the report.)

■ Text of report
- Introduction (Formal reports begin with an introduction that sets the scene and announces the subject. It gives the background, the purpose and the significance.)
- Body (The principal section in a formal report is the body. It discusses, analyzes, interprets and evaluates the research findings or solutions to the initial problem. This is where you show the evidence that justifies your conclusions.)
- Conclusions (This important section tells what the findings mean, particularly in terms of solving the initial problem.)
- Recommendations (When requested, you should submit recommendations that make precise suggestions for actions to solve the reported problem.)

■ Supplementary parts (Appendix and/or Bibliography)

③ Points to Remember

When writing a report, you'd better follow the following points which will ensure that your report be in conformity with the report style.

- Get to the point quickly. Whatever you explain, do it in a straightforward way. If appropriate, place additional information in appendices.
- Consider your readers' preference and adjust your writing style accordingly. Ask yourself the questions: should I include a glossary? Use shorter sentences? Use more headings?
- Create a professional image. Demonstrate the following characteristics will help you present yourself as a professional:
  * Be cooperative. Mind your language and tone to make readers clear that your goal is to solve a problem.
  * Be moderate in your judgments and be modest. The problem you are describing will not likely make your organization fall down overnight. The solution you propose will not solve all the company's problems. Keep a modest tone and

acknowledge that you don't know everything.
* Be fair. Acknowledging the strengths of opposing points of view makes you seen as broad-minded and aware of the complexity of the issue and so ultimately as more intelligent, reliable and credible.

☞ **B. Experience by reading and answering questions.**

a. Read the following report and answer the questions.
- *How many parts does the body of a report usually consist of? What are they?*
- *What is the cause of the decline in sales of Shanghai Branch?*

To: Mile Johnson, Sales Manager
From: Sarah Lee
Date: October 9, 2020
Subject: Sales Performance of the Shanghai Branch

Introduction
　Following your instruction, we examined the cause of the decline in sales of Shanghai Branch. We visited the office and most of their major customers there. These are my findings.

Findings
- Some of the major customers in Shanghai have closed down, and some have moved to other areas.
- Other customers are planning to move to new Suzhou or Wuxi as business there is booming and they can enjoy favorable policy from the local government there.
- The Shanghai Office has not kept an up-to-date mailing list for sending circulars to existing customers who have moved out of Shanghai, or to potential customers moving in.

Conclusions
　◇ A more favorable after-sales mix is needed to keep our customers there.
　◇ An up-to-date mailing list for sending circulars should be made.

Recommendations
　Upon the basis of the above findings and the conclusions, I recommend:
- ♦ A traveling sales representative be positioned in Shanghai as this person will keep contact with customers who have moved out of Shanghai but may still purchase our goods.
- ♦ Technical support be given in Shanghai Branch to deal with information or data sorting.

---

b. Read the following report and answer the questions.
- *How is the opening of the report?*
- *How is the "Content and Benefits" part written?*

Report on Recommendation for a One-day Training Session

Introduction
　The aim of this report is to recommend a one-day training session called "Familiarity with Your Post" for the sales representatives of the Sales Department.

Reasons

We have recruited several sales representatives recently. In spite of former sales experience, they are not familiar with their new working environment and may need quite a period to adapt to everything. Such a one-day training session seems to be necessary and urgent.

Contents and Benefits

There are many items relevant to the one-day training session for the sales representatives, which is designed to highlight work efficiency in the company.

Some brief information of the company should be given, such as the company's history, its organizational structure and financial structure. The current situation of the company should be emphasized too. These would probably develop their loyalty and affection to the company.

They must be informed of the company's main products, its annual sales volume, and the sales target of this year. Clear recognition of this can help them adjust their personal goals and it will be served as great motivation.

Then, the course can focus on our customers. High value should be put on the types and characteristics of the target customers. Their needs are also expected to be transmitted to the sales representatives, which will help them to be more responsive and adaptive when selling products.

They should be given a brief introduction to the people whom they are working together with since coordination and teamwork can greatly contribute to the company.

Recommendations

We strongly recommend that training be arranged as soon as possible. And it could not be held on weekends, or it may occupy their spare time.

15.1.2 Practice

A. Read the notes and write a report to the Local Council, telling the results given below and making the following recommendations.

<u>Attacks from white sharks since last September</u>

1) Ten incidents occurred along the local beach.
2) Five people were killed including one eight-year boy.
3) Nine people were injured.
4) This month, white sharks broke through safety chain of baths several times.

<u>Recommendations</u>

1) Place warning signs in prominent positions
2) Install a safety chain across the ocean end of the baths
3) Install a loudspeaker system
4) Store safety and rescue equipment in an accessible position

Unit 15 Business Reports

☞ **B. Read and complete the following report according to the Chinese given in the brackets.**

Introduction

_____①_____ (此报告旨在) to recommend a supplier for our new range of leisure wear. A committee from the Purchasing Department was presented with a short list of five potential suppliers to select from. The criteria considered were price, quality, delivery, and flexibility.

Findings

It was found that, _____②_____ (对这些公司的总体评价结果加以考虑), there was negligible difference among suppliers. Consequently, the committee decided to narrow their focus to the areas considered to be of major importance for Quay West's range, namely quality and price.

Consort Trading: Despite offering the best deal financially, the company is unable to guarantee garments compliant with EU standards.

Smokovska: Although it produces goods of an extremely high quality for exclusive markets, this supplier charges high price, part of which would necessarily be passed on to customers.

Namlong Sportswear: _____③_____ (较差的工艺标准) make it difficult to justify paying the price quoted.

Shiva Trading: Sample items from this supplier show an acceptable quality level. Furthermore, the deals currently on offer make it an attractive option.

Hai Xin Group: There are some doubts as to whether garments produced by this company would meet EU standards. In view of this, the prices appear unreasonably high.

Conclusion

It was felt to be unwise to risk compromising the company's image by using suppliers of low quality. Similarly, using an expensive supplier could affect Quay West's reputation for value for money. So Shiva Trading seems to be _____④_____ (最合适做我们的供货商).

☞ **C. Read the following sentences and rearrange them under the different headings of the following report.**

Sentences available for rearranging a report:

1) Despite the merger rumours, any investment in Bute Chemicals would involve a risk. Ramsden, on the other hand, despite its present inefficiency, is still profitable and has definite potential for further growth.

2) We would recommend investment in Ramseden Breweries.

3) This report aims to assess which company, either Ramsden Breweries or Bute Chemicals, we should invest in.

4) The company had mixed results last year; although turnover increased by approximately 25%, net profit rose by less than 4%. However, restructuring may be able to eliminate these inefficiencies and expected growth in the drinks industry

suggests opportunities for increased profits.

5) Results were disappointing, with turnover and profit both falling slightly. Nevertheless, the company managed to increase its dividend to shareholders. The rumoured merger seems likely to push up the share price considerably.

Report on Investment Potential of Ramsden Breweries and Bute Chemicals
Introduction
...
Ramsden
...
Bute
...
Conclusion
...
Recommendation
...

15.1.3 Case study & practice

Write a report on the topic of "Satisfaction with Employee Benefits" to Mr Aihua Chen, Director of Personnel.

You will first gather some information from employees at different levels in the company. Obtaining such information may involve looking through the past files regarding this problem. It may involve interviewing employees from different levels. Next you will analyze the situation in light of all you have learned about it. Then you will develop some recommendations to the situation. You may want to investigate the following aspects:

- Overall satisfaction
- Problem when dealing with the personnel department
- Suggestions for improvement
- Problems when dealing with HMO (Health Maintenance Organization)

15.2 Communicating & Writing Skills

☞ **A. Read the following report and learn to state what the report is about.**

An Investigation Report on Reducing Operation Cost
To: The Board of Directors
From: John Jones
Date: April 2, 2021
Following is an investigation report on reducing the operation cost of the Delivery Service Department.

Investigation including:
- An examination of all trucks and other delivery equipment.
- A study of the maintenance and operating cost of each unit in our delivery system over the past twelve months.
- An examination of the personnel.

Recommendations:
- Trade in 3 trucks for new equipment. All 3 have traveled in excess of 100,000 miles, and the maintenance cost of each prevents economical operation.
- 4 trucks should have minor overhauling to increase their efficiency.
- The towns and cities receiving delivery service on Tuesdays, Thursdays, and Saturdays should be cut only on Tuesdays and Saturdays to reduce our operating costs.

Translate the following sentences into English.

1）本报告是对改革奖金制度的可行性的评估。
2）撰写本报告的目的就是提高我们的市场份额。
3）本报告旨在对使用 Cooling 海滩的游泳者所面临的危险进行调查。
4）本报告旨在为我们的机械玩具推荐一名供货商。

☞ **B. Read the following report and learn to present the result of investigation or make recommendation.**

Report on the Introduction of New Practices

Introduction

The report sets out to describe the most attractive features of staff management policies of the HVC Garden chain restaurants and to suggest the introduction of some items into the restaurant department of our hotel. The presented information has been obtained during the Assistant Manager's visit to the HVC Garden.

Findings

It was found that one of the HVC restaurants is exposed to an exceptionally innovative management, and it has recently developed a new policy in order to maintain high standards in all aspects of the service provided to its guests. The two successful practices of the policy are as follows:

- ➢ All the waiting staff are exposed to a check-up before starting their lunch and dinner shifts so as to ensure maintenance of hygiene and compliance with the company's dress code.
- ➢ The evening briefings conducted on a regular basis in order to inform the staff of the basic changes in the menu and wine supplies have proved effective.

Conclusions

It is clear that a successful introduction of the two procedures is sure to reflect on the waiting staff's better awareness of good service and an improvement in the hotel's image.

Recommendations

It is suggested that these two procedures (staff's check-up and regular evening briefings) should be applied in the restaurant department of our hotel.

Study the following examples.

⇒ Presenting the result of investigation

1) Our research reveals ...
2) Having made a close study of the survey, I find ...
3) It is found that ...
4) This is my finding: ...

⇒ Giving necessary proposal or opinion

1) So I'd like to put forward my opinion on the matter ...
2) My opinion for your reference is ...
3) In my opinion, ...
4) I strongly hope ...

C. Read the following report and learn to draw conclusions.

A Report on Proposed Installation of Automatic Coffee Machine

From: Personnel Manager
To: Managing Director
Date: May 16, 2021
Subject: Proposed Installation of Automatic Coffee Machine

Following your memorandum of April 27, we carried out a small study of staff views in selected departments.

My personnel officer informally asked a representative sample of office workers a number of questions. He asked whether:
- they drank coffee during their break;
- they made it themselves or brought it with from home;
- they would be in favour of a shorter coffee break;
- they would use an automatic coffee machine if available.

We can summarize the results as follows:
- 65% said they enjoy a good cup of coffee;
- only 5% brought their own coffee from home;
- 25% would be in favour of a shorter coffee break and finishing earlier;
- 15% said they would use an automatic coffee machine;
- but more added: if the coffee was cheap.

On April 30, during a routine meeting with the chief union representative, I mentioned that in some departments the coffee break was lasting a lot longer than is actually allowed. The representative's answer was not very helpful. She said the union insist on the coffee break be left as it is. She also said without asking all the union members in the company their opinion, the union would not agree with any shortening of the coffee break.

In conclusion, it seems important to draw the board's attention to possible difficulties which the rapid installation of coffee machine could bring.

In my opinion, we need to discuss the problem a little longer and with more people before taking any action, and we should work out a solution with the help from the union.

Ronald Greenfield

Complete the following sentences by choosing the expressions given in the box.

| conclusion | conclusions | sum up | It is clear that |

1) To _____, my investigation indicates that investment in the ABC Company is not as reliable or beneficial as investment in the field we have been engaged in.
2) In _____, the purchase of new laptops is necessary at present.
3) _____ the English proficiency of our marketing staff is far from satisfactory.
4) No _____ were reached regarding the solution to the problem.

15.3 Writers' Workshop: Accuracy & Objectivity

Accuracy & Objectivity

The most important elements of business report writing are accuracy and objectivity.

Accuracy in business report writing means accuracy of information and that of writing. Since the information in a business report is used to make decisions, inaccurate information can lead to inaccurate decisions. Therefore, it is very important to make sure the facts are right. The accuracy of any report depends upon the correctness of the data gathered to prepare it. Sources used ought to be reliable and accurate in reporting all information.

The accuracy of writing depends on accuracy in writing mechanics (spelling, punctuation, and grammar) and accuracy in writing style.

In order to achieve the quality of seriousness, we usually adopt formal style for writing business reports. So the passive voice, sentences beginning with "it", nominalisations and long learned words are commonly seen for objectivity in business report writing.

Credibility

To enhance credibility, you ought to remember the following points:
- Avoid emotional terms
- Identify assumptions
- Label opinions
- Use documentation

15.3.1 Group work

Discuss in groups and state the purpose or the aim of the report you are to write according to the following telephone conversations.

(1)

"John, can you get that report ready for me by next Thursday? ... I want you to present an overview of the Personnel Department: you know, structure and organisation—you get the idea ... "

(2)

"Jane. Don't forget the weekly sales report is due on Friday—usual sort of thing—product progress update, survey of week's events in the market. Look forward to seeing it on my desk on Friday then."

(3)

"Peter, I read your report last night—very interesting. I particularly liked the part where you presented the results of your interviews—I'd never have guessed that the man in the street would prefer to see less rather than more television. Also, your findings as regards favourite programme type were quite eye-opening."

(4)

"Lorna. That report you sent me yesterday. Are you sure you can conclude from your limited evidence that this company should expand into the European market? I mean, surely we need to look at our potential competitors' activities very closely before we can do that with any confidence."

15.3.2 Rewriting the following sentences to make them more formal in style

1) I am glad to enclose a check for you.
2) I am glad to tell you that your application for a post as a secretary was successful.
3) I am sorry to tell you that we cannot deliver the goods on time.
4) Could you tell me your prices?
5) Here is our invoice.

15.3.3 Comment and improvement

Comment on the following report and make improvement.

> So far, a total of 12 government-driven industrial zones are reported to have been in operation in the northern Jiangsu regions, jointly funded and administered by one of southern Jiangsu provincial cities and one of their sister cities in northern Jiangsu area. This move is highly encouraged by the Provincial Government, designed to take advantage of the pressing needs for existing manufacturing businesses in the increasingly overcrowded and polluted cities in the south to those northern Jiangsu regions, hungry for industrial capitals and new jobs.
>
> Since 2006, Jiangsu Provincial Government has encouraged its southern cities to partner with their northern counterparts in the financing and operation of industrial zones in the underdeveloped northern Jiangsu, which is still blessed with abundant resources of labor, land, environment load capacity. Major industrial cities in the south were also quick to recognize the benefit of this policy as they are faced with the hard choice of having to push out some redundant or low-end manufacturing capacity. By September 2008, some 6,770 cases of investments have been transferred from the south to the north, mainly located in the newly co-sponsored industrial zones. Experts noticed that a lion's share of such businesses are involved in the heavily polluting industries such as chemicals, textile printing and dyeing, metal plating and so on. Investigation shows the reason for industrial relocation includes the following:
> - Southern cities are running out of usable land resources, especially since 2006 when the central

government tightens up industrial land quota and its offering requirements.
- Accumulated environment pollution in these cities is badly reported and believed to endanger the life of the people.
- Low-end manufacturing industries are on the edge of losing money or forced to close down, due to their increasing cost in terms of labor, land acquisition, environmental protection and others.
- Northern cities, on the contrary, are blessed with abundant resources but are in hungry of manufacturing business and employment opportunities.
- Significant cost savings and more administrative incentives are negotiable with the governments in the northern region, thanks to their desire to introduce various types of industries.

To strike a balance of economic benefits and environmental protection, some recommendations are given as follows:
- Map out strategic planning for co-sponsored industrial zones and identify targeted industries.
- Encourage concentration of industrial businesses in industry-specific industrial zones to share common utilities and infrastructure for the maximization of output.
- Put in place environmental protection facilities such as waste-water treatment works, solid and gaseous disposal facilities, and heavy metal disposal facilities.
- Enhance entry requirements to screen potential investments and minimize potential pollution risks for incoming businesses.

1. List of Long & Short Words

Long Words	Short Words
acknowledge	admit, thank
advise	tell, say
anticipate	expect
alleviate	lessen, ease
aggregate	total
ameliorate	improve
application	use
commence	start, begin
consequence	result, outcome
deem	consider, believe
demonstrate	show
enable	allow, help
endeavour	try
Esteemed Sir	Dear Sir
expedite	rush
eventuality	result, outcome
facilitate	help, aid
forward	send
immediately	now
implement	start
initiate	start, begin
kindly	please
necessitate	require
notwithstanding	but, despite, regardless
obligation	duty

(continuous)

Long Words	Short Words
objective	aim, goal
occurrence	event, incident
perusal	review, information
purchase	buy
signify	mean
subsequent	after
substantial	large
substantiate	support, prove
terminate	end
utilize	use
variation	change

2. List of Obsolete & Popular Expressions

Obsolete Expressions	Popular Expressions
as per your request	as you request
acknowledge receipt of	have received
as to	about/concerning/regarding
as stated above	as I said
awaiting the favour of your early response	I look forward to hearing from you soon
avail oneself of	use
at this time / at the present time	now / at present
by means of	by
cheque to cover	cheque for
comply with our request	do as we request
dated October 10	of October 10
due to the fact that / for the reason that	because
enclosed herewith please find	we enclose
favour, communication	letter, memo, fax
few and far between	seldom
for the purpose of	for
I am in receipt of	Thank you for / I have received
if it is within our power	if we can

(continuous)

Obsolete Expressions	Popular Expressions
in accordance with / as per	according to
in advance of / prior to	before
in view of	because of
in a position to	be able to
in the near future	soon
in this day and age	nowadays
in the event of	if
in some cases	sometimes
inform me of the reason	tell me why
in connection with	about
party	person
pursuant to / subsequent to	after
pertaining to	of, about, concerning
Please be good / kind enough to advise us ...	Please tell us ...
the undersigned / the writer	I/me/we
the vast majority of	most of
under no circumstances	never
under separate cover	separately
up to this writing	until now
We beg to inform you ...	I am writing to inform you ...
with reference to / with regard to / with respect to	about/regarding/concerning/relating to

3. List of Redundant & Concise Expressions

Redundant Expressions	Concise Expressions
absolutely perfect	perfect
actual experience	experience
a great honour and a privilege	an honour
as a general rule	as a rule
arrive at the conclusion	conclude
at a later date	later
at an early date	soon/immediately
at your earliest convenience	soon / as soon as possible

(continuous)

Redundant Expressions	Concise Expressions
as to whether	whether
advance warning/plan	warning/plan
completely eliminate	eliminate
during the year that	during
enclosed with	enclosed
exactly identical	identical
perfectly clear	clear
few in number	few
personal opinion	opinion
basic essentials	essentials
be of the opinion	believe/think
close proximity	near
continue on	continue
current status	status
contributing factor	factor
forward by mail	send
free of charge	free
group meeting	meeting
in a manner similar to	like
inasmuch as	as
in the matter of	about
in the amount of	for
in the course of	during
in order to	to
in spite of the fact that	although
of even date	today
of recent date	recent
of yesterday's date	yesterday
on behalf of	for
place emphasis on	emphasize
put in an appearance	appear

(continuous)

Redundant Expressions	Concise Expressions
please don't hesitate to	please
send an answer	reply
so as to	to
until such time as you can	until you can
visible to the eye	visible
integral part	part
collect together	collect
whether or not	if
with a view to	to
with the exception of	except
with the object of	to

References

Bird, B. *High Speed Business Writing*(商务信函写作实务)[M]. 张亦辉,译. 北京:外语教学与研究出版社,2006.

Ellis, M. & Johnson, C. *Teaching Business English* [M]. Shanghai:Shanghai Foreign Language Education Press, 2002.

Gartside, L. *English Business Studies* [M]. Plymouth:Macdonald & Evans Ltd, 1989.

Jones, L. & Alexander, R. *New International Business English*(剑桥国际商务英语)[M]. 北京:华夏出版社,2001.

Lindsell,R. *Writing Business Letters for Dummies*(商务信函写作)[M]. 北京:机械工业出版社,2004.

Littlejohn, A. *A Communicative Approach to Business Correspondence in English*(剑桥商务英语写作教程)[M].陈荣,译注. 北京:北京大学出版社,2000.

Roddick,H. *Business Writing Makeovers*(如何写出完美的商务英语信函)[M]. 郁震,等译.上海:上海世界图书出版公司,2005.

Taylor, S. *Model Business Letters, E-mails & Other Business Documents*(商务英语写作实例精解)[M]. 张卫平,译.北京:外语教学与研究出版社,2007.

Watson, J. *Business Writing Basics*(商务英语写作指南)[M]. 鲁刚,译.上海:上海世界图书出版公司,2004.

贝内特. 从零开始网络英语[M]. 北京:中国大百科全书出版社,2004.

冯祥春. 外经贸英语函电[M]. 北京:对外经济贸易大学出版社,2003.

甘鸿. 外经贸英语函电[M]. 上海:上海科学技术文献出版社,1996.

管春林. 国际商务英语写作[M]. 杭州:浙江大学出版社,2006.

何光明. 新国际商务英语写作[M]. 上海:上海教育出版社,2005.

雷春林. 商务英语写作教程[M]. 北京:对外经济贸易大学出版社,2008.

李太志. 商务英语言语修辞艺术[M]. 北京:国防工业出版社,2006.

李太志. 商务英语写作实训[M]. 北京:国防工业出版社,2008.

李太志. 商务英语写作修辞的对比研究[M]. 上海:上海外语教育出版社,2009.

莫再树. 商务英语写作[M]. 北京:国防工业出版社,2006.

滕美荣. 现代商务英语写作[M]. 北京:首都经济贸易大学出版社,2007.

翁凤翔. 文本写作[M]. 杭州:浙江大学出版社,2002.

朱慧萍. 商务英语写作[M]. 北京:首都经济贸易大学出版社,2008.